Guangzhou

Heart of the South

Lindsey Bard – GZTraveler

Guangzhou – Heart of the South

Text, cover image and time line are copyright © 2014 Lindsey Bard

All Rights Reserved. No part of this work may be reproduced without written permission of the author, except for brief quotations used in reviews or critical articles.

This book is a work of nonfiction. People, places and events as presented are not reproduction or composites.

Lindsey Bard
Sanford, NC 27332
gztravelguide@gmail.com

Please visit the website www.gztraveler.weebly.com for more information, videos and pictures of these sites.

Bard

Guangzhou – Heart of the South

Dedication

Many people helped me achieve this goal, but a few names stand out in particular.

The volunteers/hosts – who selflessly gave of their time and insights, were willing to work around my schedule and speak in public in a language not native to them. None of this could have been accomplished without their help.

Mom – who has always been proud of me.

Dad – who fed my love of history.

My students and co-workers at GZ4 – who shared their stories, some of which made it into this book as casual references or places to start my research.

Wally K. – who encouraged me to chase my dream, despite the high cost we paid.

Jon G. – who went walkabout to all these places with me first.

Prof. Brad King – who helped me crystallize my idea for the project.

Prof. Mary Spillman – who was willing to work with a student she had never met on a project she was given only the vaguest outline for and the tightest schedule.

Scott B. – who made it seem so easy, the bardic rat.

Josh B. – who helped me stay sane through the process.

Vader – who is the best of all possible Vaders and friends.

Amanda J. – who lent her great wisdom and talent with a red pen.

Max the Magnificent and Persephone the Huntress – who provided company and support at the finish line in their own fuzzy ways.

Guangzhou – Heart of the South

Table of Contents

Introduction

Chapter 1 – Chen Clan Academy

Chapter 2 – Guangdong Museum

Chapter 3 – Museum of the Nanyue King of the Western Han Dynasty

Chapter 4 – Temples of Yuexiu district

Chapter 5 – Yuexiu Park

Chapter 6 – Baiyun Mountain Reserve

Chapter 7 – Chimelong Safari Park

Works Cited and References

Timeline of Guangdong and Southern China

This timeline begins with the Qin Dynasty, not the beginning of China's history. Instead, it starts at the point where Guangdong entered China's history.

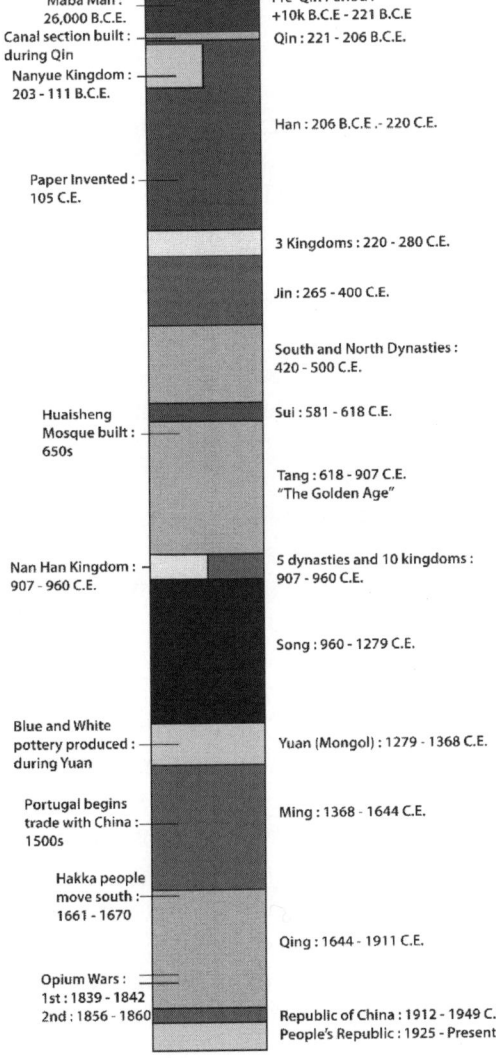

Introduction

Welcome to Guangzhou and Canton and Panyu. The city has changed its name at least three times over the centuries, and the people have changed with it. It's known as the City of Flowers for the historic flower markets that fill the city in the spring and the City of Rams or Goats based on its foundation story. A hub of business for more than 2,000 years as a major point for the Maritime Silk Road trade, it's the central city of the South. This guide will delve into some of the history and explore a few of the notable sites alongside the people who call Guangzhou home.

Guangzhou is a city of hidden gems. Each district in the older sections of town has a museum tucked around a corner. The newer sections of town have modern, larger facilities for art and music presentations. This is the home of Cantonese Opera and the oldest Islamic mosque in China. Neither the city nor the province it's the capital of brag a lot, but they have plenty to be proud of.

Guangzhou is settled in the basin of the Zhujiang River, a region which has seen human habitation for more than 10,000 years. Neolithic tribes hunted, fished, gathered and grew food and prospered. Several tombs and burial sites from this period were discovered in Guangdong in the mid-1900's. These finds have spurred ongoing archaeological digs sponsored by the local and national government. Pottery shards, burial vessels and skeletal remains are now part of the displays in several museums around the city.

By 206 B.C.E, Guangzhou was well-established as the capital of the Nanyue Empire under the name Panyu, so named for the nearby mountains Pan and Yu. This city center is where the modern districts of eastern Yuexiu and northern Liwan are now. During the height of Nanyue's imperial power, it spread its control over the whole Guangdong region, much of southern China and down into what is today Vietnam. In 111 B.C.E, the Nanyue Empire was fully adsorbed into the Han dynasty[1]. This marked the beginning of a joint north-south history often marred by rebellions. The unequal partnership between these two still influences the region and Guangzhou.

During the Nanyue period, the Guangdong province came to be known as Kuang-tong meaning "Wide East" with the province to its west "Kuang-hsi" "Wide West". This romanized spelling of the Chinese characters is most likely why Westerners traveling to the region called the area Canton, not understanding that the pronunciation is closer to Guangdong. Though the territory of Guangdong has shrunk since the Nanyue Empire, it still covers 69,400sq.mi (179,800sq.km) an area larger than Uruguay with Guangzhou as its capital city[2].

Guangzhou is the largest city in the south of China, dwarfing Hong Kong both in size and population by several magnitudes. A 2010 census placed the city's population at just under 13 million people; in 2014 estimates range from 14 to 17 million living in the city. To contrast, Australia's 2014 population is estimated to be 23.6 million people. If the local satellite city of Foshan is added to Guangzhou's, the population of these two cities equals or exceeds Australia's population[3].

Today, Guangzhou is the third largest city in China and a major import and export hub welcoming thousands of travelers and business people, especially in the spring and fall when the Canton Trade Fair takes place[4]. The people here boast of their food – dim sum being the calling card of the region – but rarely of their own history. Massive growth and development in the past thirty years has seen Guangzhou more than triple its city footprint. The modern central business district, where the iconic Canton Tower (called Guangzhou Tower by the locals) and other skyscrapers now sit, was farmland at the start of the 1980s[5][6]. Now a modern subway systems connects Baiyun Airport in the north with Panyu District in the south and delivers passengers throughout the city within a few minutes.

The city is again flexing its trade hub muscles, but is often overlooked as a travel destination despite being the birthplace of the modern Chinese government and home to numerous museums and historic sites. This oversight has been in part due to close proximity to Hong Kong and Macao. Both cities have been easier to enter due to their more relaxed visa policies. Nor has Guangzhou pushed itself into the public eye in the way that Beijing with its Great Wall and palaces has. It has chosen instead to focus on business and is only now revealing its cultural value to the world.

The southern region, culture and people are often referred to as Lingnan, a reference to the mountain range that divides the south from the north of China[7]. Lingnan culture is distinctly different from the northern Mandarin tradition with the most noticeable example being the language. People here usually learn Cantonese as their first language and Mandarin, northern Chinese, in school. Cantonese and Lingnan can be thought of as synonymous. The name Canton, adopted by the Western world, was used to refer to both the Guangdong province and the city of Guangzhou.

"Northern people think Cantonese is just a dialect. We

know it's a different language," said Cecilia, a study adviser at a local English learning center. This can present some difficulties for travelers, even those who know Mandarin. They may discover that their taxi cab driver doesn't understand them when they give directions. To add to the confusion, some residents learned a different local dialect before they moved from their small hometown to the big city. Cecilia speaks one of these dialects. She says she comes from a small town, only a million people. There is no written form of Cantonese or any of the other dialects of Chinese, all movies and TV programs are subtitled in Mandarin. That way everyone, regardless of what they speak, can understand the show.

Since English has become the business world's lingua franca, most people below the age of twenty-five are at least partially fluent. English lessons begin in kindergarten, and many companies encourage their employees to improve their skills in order to attain promotions. Older residents of the city or those who have recently moved to the city may not have such a strong grasp of English. It is not uncommon for a Westerner to walk down the street in an older part of town and hear "Hello" shouted at them by a man on a motorized bicycle taxi but this doesn't mean the driver has broad language skills.

For ease of travel around the city, visitors are encouraged to carry cards written in Mandarin or pictures of maps with Mandarin translations of the places they want to visit. Many hotels offer guests small cards with "Please take me to…" which they are happy to fill in for their guests. The other side of the card usually features the name of the hotel with a similar request.

Travelers should always carry their passport. The Chinese government requires that all foreigners have their passports with them at all times, and copies aren't good enough. Groups of police officers can and do spot check hotels, apartment buildings and restaurant areas. It is possible to be fined or jailed for failure to present this document when asked. Happily, having a passport is sometimes all that is needed to enter some local museums, including two featured in this book.

"Be prepared," isn't just for Boy Scouts. Visitors should consider having a little package of tissues on hand for the toilets. They can be bought at almost any shop. Western facilities are not the norm around the city, even in the newer buildings. Providing toilet paper in stalls or soap at the wash station is equally uncommon. Most shops and restaurants don't have their own toilet facilities, so travelers should not plan on "ducking in" for an emergency stop.

There is no specific order in which this guide must be read; go directly to a site of interest or read it cover-to-cover. These seven sites have been chosen for their cultural value, interest, fun and insight into China and the Southern Chinese people. Some are old and showcase the history of the region; some are modern and focus on the issues facing today's society. Their order is based on the amount of time it takes to see each site, starting with approximately two hours for Chen Clan Academy and ending with Chimelong Safari Park which takes all day.

Readers will notice that in each chapter a different Chinese host is featured. To understand the importance of a place it is best to ask those who live there, because they have the best stories. Each of these men and women volunteered to visit a site and share their experiences as a cultural insider. The hosts are native Chinese speakers who have various levels of English mastery. If they made any small grammatical errors while explaining themselves that should be overlooked. Using a foreign language is difficult, but to this was added the discomfort of public speaking. Each host is the star of a video of the visit which can be viewed at www.gztraveler.weebly.com, the companion website for this book. Photos and maps for each of these sites are also available on the website.

The hosts come from all walks of life and backgrounds. Chilli and Kay are both young women in their twenties who work together at an English language school. Kay is loud and self-deprecating, while Chilli is quiet and serious. April and Jason are university students with very different dreams. Jason wants to leave China as soon as he can and be a party boy in a more Western country. April plans to stay near her parents. Sharp-tongued Emily is in her late thirties and studies English to see her friends at the school. Vicky doesn't know much about the city's history. She has to read the signs like other tourists since she grew-up in Canada, but she has family stories which make her voice worth hearing. Her family is from Guangzhou and she wants to reconnect with her hometown. Wilson eagerly volunteered and was glad to go back to the mountain. He's in his mid-forties and a bit nostalgic for his earlier life when things weren't so fast-paced. Tracy is married and she and her husband take groups on planned holidays. After her tour of Chimelong she rushed to meet one of these groups heading to Hong Kong for a long weekend.

There is one further host found in this book: Mrs. Henry Gray. In 1880, she published her personal correspondence with her mother as *Fourteen Months in Canton*. Mrs. Gray lived in Guangzhou with her husband, the Anglican Archdeacon John Henry Gray, M.A., from early 1877 to late 1878. As was common in that time, she often wrote to her mother about her experiences in the region. The Guangzhou she saw and the city that exists today are not the same, but there are parts that she would recognize.

Guangzhou – Heart of the South

She admits that she finds some of the Chinese customs and habits difficult to understand and occasionally silly. She is a product of her time and culture: a British woman living in a small European enclave and part of the culture that recently defeated the Chinese in the Opium Wars. She refers to the British and French as "the allies" instead of the aggressors. The habit for British writers at this time was to thoroughly denigrate the Chinese in their writings. Mrs. Gray chose a different tone in her letters and paints a more balanced and thorough picture of the city she walked almost daily with her husband. She even includes comments about how silly her fellow Europeans were for not getting to know the local people better[8].

Her insights can offer a deeper understanding of the city as it used to be. In her time in the city she met Chinese leaders and fine ladies whom she greatly admired. She helped one girl learn English and always felt bad for not speaking enough Chinese. She gave birth to twins, a boy and girl, which earned her a great deal of honor and praise from the Chinese community. The family survived a typhoon that destroyed part of their house and killed neighbors. She and her husband were active members of the Chinese community. The family left Guangzhou when Mrs. Gray's health started to fail and she had to return to England for treatment.

Her letters in this book are out of sequence. Each was chosen because it has some connection to the site discussed in that chapter. No redactions have been made to her letters, though only seven of the more than forty that she wrote are included here. Her grammar and spelling choices have been maintained throughout. Mrs. Gray did not publish her signature at the ends of her letters, so "Your loving daughter" and her first name – never mentioned in her book – are likewise not included here nor are her illustrations. Her book

Fourteen Months in Canton is now in the public domain and available for free in a variety of formats for readers who wish to learn more about her and her life in the City of Rams.

Welcome to Guangzhou.

- GZTraveler

Chapter 1 – Chen Clan Academy

Chen Clan Academy and the Guangdong Folk Art Museum

How to get there: Take metro Line 6 to Chen Clan Academy stop exit D then turn right.

How much: 10 RMB per guest, one day a month is free. Guests over 65 get in free.

How long: 1-3 hours

In the heart of Liwan district stands the former home-away-from-home residence for members of the Chen family. Today it is the Guangdong Folk Art Museum. It was built between 1888-1893 during the Guangxu Reign of the Qing Dynasty, twenty years after the Second Opium war[1]. Chilli, a Chen family member in her early twenties, points out that in this region Chen is one of the most common family names – the southern Chinese equivalent of Smith. Her grandfather tells her stories about this house, and she takes a special pride in it as part of her family legacy.

The complex covers 49,212sq.ft (15,000sq.m) including the exterior and interior courtyards. The house's floor space is 21,000sq.ft (6,400sq.m)[2]. It was built using the principles of symmetry and following Feng shui traditions. The money to build the house was raised when seventy-two of the clan branches donated to the construction fund. Many of the branches of the family didn't live in the city. Some had even made their fortunes in other countries, but they sent money back to build this house[3]. This helped ensure that their sons would be allowed to enter and study here and that they would have access to the site used for ancestor veneration.

Guangzhou has been the capital of the southern region of China for the past 2,000 years[4]. This made it the seat of government and trade, but also the location for yearly imperial examinations which could lead to government jobs. Any male member of the seventy-two clans who wished to study for and take the exams could reside in the family house[5]. Passing the examination was difficult and if achieved bestowed great honor on the entire family.

Each of the families was given a map of the city with the house marked and distances from Guangzhou were noted in the corner. This was to help make travel planning easier for members living in distant cities or countries. A copy of one of these maps is posted in a display at the back of the house. Chilli says, "It's just like a very useful map and includes transportation information made back in 1888. At that time people walked or they came here riding horses." She laughs when she notices a local landmark drawn in. For this older section of the town the map would still guide travelers around the city effectively.

The basic length of study for a young man was two years, with testing done on a three year cycle. Examination years one and two were the equivalent of a bachelor's degree, and would make the examinee eligible for lower government positions. In year three, the master's degree equivalent was tested – the highest possible educational achievement[6]. Students were allowed to retest year after year. The small number of students allowed to pass each year was set by the government based on population numbers in the provinces and the number of open government positions available. This meant that every year thousands of hopeful students would test and a hundred or two might pass[7][8]. Some students would never find success.

Today, university students are expected to focus their studies in one or two major areas, but during the examination period studies covered math, science and other subjects, though the greatest emphasis was placed on understanding of classic literature. All of these subjects had to be mastered and could be on the exam[9][10]. In 1905, the government abolished the 1,500 year-old practice of examination placements in an attempt to provide modernizing changes and quell rising dissent among the literati[11]. The dissent continued, but the system was finished. The Chen school continued for several more years afterwards and its use as a school during this time accounts for one of its many names, the Chen Family Calligraphy School[12].

The Chen house also served as a hotel for family traveling through the area and as a central gathering point for family events and festivals. If there was any business that the family needed to discuss, they could gather in the front hall and discuss it in privacy and comfort; alternately, they could go out into the city to deal with government issues.

The Chen home was not the only of its kind in the city. Most of the large families had a similar compound and several survive around the city, but this is one of the largest and features the best preserved examples of rooftop decorations and other art features[13].

When the government was given the building in the 1950's, it became the Folk Crafts Museum of Guangdong. Today it has the largest grouping of traditional architecture and home decorative folk art in the province[14]. "I like it very much, because I can see a lot of different kinds of art forms here, and some of them I can't see outside of Chen Clan Academy," says Chilli. The artwork on display is always changing and the decorations on the roof beams could be looked at for hours without noticing all the details.

Standing outside the house Chilli takes time to look at the carved gray brickwork set into the walls. This is an art not found outside the southern region[15]. There are side entrances, but most visitors move towards the large main entrance doors. Stone Fu dogs or lions are placed on either side of the door. These dogs are found in one form or another throughout the East Asian world. They started out as temple guards protecting the Buddha, or Fu, and now protect any important building. The female will always have a baby lion under her paw showing that she protects the weak, while the male will have a ball representing his duty to guard the world.

Chilli stops just inside the entrance and examines the doors. They are guarded by the traditional gods of the home. The two great warriors painted in bright greens and pinks are based on a story of two generals who protected the emperor one night, scaring away demons and angry ghosts[16]. For centuries, their images have been painted on doorways to protect the family inside from evil and harm. The two-and-a-half meter high, solid wood doors on which the fierce gods are painted were hand carved and are swung open each morning to welcome visitors. Guests hold their cameras high to take photos of the snarling faces. If these spiritual warriors didn't cause people in the crowded streets of 1890 to avert their gaze into the house, the large carved wooden panels set just inside the door provided privacy for the family.

These heavy, dark wood panels stretch floor to ceiling and feature detailed carvings of tea services, chickens with their young and intricate lattice work. This style of wood work continues throughout the house. "You can imagine, there are too many carvings...a lot of small tiny holes... There would be a lot of cleaning ladies, they would start from maybe three or four in the morning and then maybe by the evening they would finish," says Chilli after admiring the panels for several minutes.

Today, the staff tends to let the areas above seven feet collect dust for days or weeks instead of climbing ladders to clean. Ceilings in some of the areas stretch more than thirty-two feet high (10m) with decorations all the way up. It's easy to see why the staff might not wish to spend all their time polishing a carved chicken head twenty feet off the ground. The style of wood carving is an art found in the northern parts of Guangdong. Screens throughout the house show off the artists' skills at storytelling and delicate craft work. Illustrations from famous stories and historical events are completed in minute detail on the many panels[17].

Once through the main entrance visitors spread out. There is a help desk in the corner of the entrance hall where brochures and maps of the house are available in a variety of languages. No set direction or path through the house is laid out. Guests are encouraged to wander through the exhibits at their leisure or sit in the courtyards and relax. It's common to see a small tour group pass an old man lounging in one of the chairs or a pair of university students discussing a project in the courtyard at a table under a tree.

The house is a large square divided in the middle by a long gallery room. The side wall areas are where the families or bachelors would live and the men would study[18]. Corridors here are open-sided covered walkways, with square courtyards in between bisecting pathways. Each walkway and roof beam is covered in lime-based plaster art, paintings, or ceramic sculpture works. Tiny colorful plaster families gather together to listen to an elder speak or a group of young men stand around a table while a teacher reviews a point. They are found among the birds, fish, and other animals covering the walls. One roof ridge displays an entire village of tiny people and houses.

When the sun shines, these painted wall pieces light up with lucky red, bold yellow, grass green and other bright colors against the backdrop of the dark green ceramic tiles. These tiles are seen on many of the older buildings in the city and countryside. They were produced in the pottery kilns in Foshan and are a staple of the local ceramic tradition[19].

Chilli points to some of the figures, "They tell stories," she says. "They will teach children to be polite and treat their families in a good way," others offer hope for long life. Ceramic tables and barrel chairs are placed at the corners of the walkways and in the courtyards so visitors can sit and look at the art. Families gather for afternoon tea, and a group of elderly men come down each day to meet and talk at one table in the front courtyard. Birds sing here, something of a novelty in the heart of this metropolis.

When the house was first turned over to the government, art historians and restorers were called in to assess the house and the art. They contacted traditional artists in the area, some of whom are the descendants of the original artists who helped build the house. Together they determined the best way to repair and preserve the home[8]. "I believe there's a very important concept about repairing the old things... We try to keep it the way they are instead of making it modern or too brand new. That gives the wrong idea," Chilli says. She spent her first year at university studying to do this sort of work; her roommate completed the program and is in Italy learning restoration techniques.

Conservation and restoration efforts can be viewed in the side gallery near the entrance which highlights the damage the building's exterior art suffered over the years and steps taken to ensure its continued place as a beautiful example of Lingnan architecture. Southern cultural, commonly called Lingnan, blends the regional mountain style of architecture, art, food and language with the lower river-basin style and is found notably in Guangdong, Guangxi, Hunan, Jiangxi and Hainan provinces and northern Vietnam[20][21]. It favors open air areas that encourage air flow, heavy shade, and tall ceilings due to the generally warm climate. Bright colors and roof decorations are also part of this style.

Next to the conservation gallery is the study hall at the end of the southwest corridor. The entrance of the room is decorated with wood carvings of grapes and cranes. The room features a long table and smaller seating arrangements as well as calligraphy pieces on the walls extolling the students to focus on their work. Visitors are not allowed into the room and rooms north of this area are closed to the public.

East of the entrance is the living quarters display. Furniture in these divided room areas is meant to show common living arrangements when the house was first built[22]. A living room, a study with desk and writing instruments and a bedroom with a heavy wooden bed and a traditional ceramic pillow make an appearance. The block pillows were designed to support the neck while not messing up the hair-styles favored in the past. They also stay cool in the heat of the sub-tropical nights and don't attract fleas. "How did they sleep with those? They look uncomfortable," says Kay, a local woman who lives a few blocks from the house. She has never visited it before. She admits that she thought it was just an old house, nothing special. Only now does she realize it's a museum. She goes into every room and through every store, laughing when she sees plastic kids' toys on the shelves.

Around the house, the maintenance staff, dressed in

their green jumpsuits, are always busy. A woman drags a heavy hose from plant to potted plant in the courtyard, watering each one as a flute plays in the background. Two women polish the red glass panes that line the wall between the corridor and the living quarter's exhibit. The glass is a special type made by local blowers[23]. The wall is made of a series of one square foot panes each seemingly etched or cut with floral patterns. Farther along, a woman with a polishing rag pauses to speak to another caretaker as she passes. She's working in the ancestral hall polishing the ceiling-high wood panels. Each of these caretakers works tirelessly to maintain the house against polluted rain, dust and dirt from the city and general wear from age and the passing of so many people through the rooms.

The central gallery is home to an ever-changing display of ceramic artwork. The pieces are selected based on a theme and changed every two to three months[24]. Ceramics and porcelain production helped develop and shape Guangzhou and the surrounding area. The satellite city of Foshan used to fire more than a hundred dragon kilns to produce the desired quantity of porcelain for export to Britain and other Western nations[25]. Today, Foshan fires only one kiln. Much of what is on display here was produced in the last fifty years[26]. "This one reminds me of those really small army men that we used to play with as kids," says Kay as she passes a display case filled with inch-tall porcelain men.

At the far back of the house is the ancestral hall. It's a long room with an open front. At the back of the room are very steep, red bleachers that reach to the ceiling surrounded by heavy, dark wood-carved panels. What's missing from these bleachers are the wooden placards that held the names of the Chen members who brought honor to the family. This is the ancestral hall of worship. The Chinese believed that relatives from the past who brought honor to the family could help present generations gain similar status[27]. They also served as a reminder that no one achieves greatness alone; everyone is aided by the family and are expected to help the family in return.

Chilli explains that if a notable member died the next of kin could pay an amount of money to have that person's name placed on a tablet in the hall. How much money was paid and how notable the family member was would determine the location of the tablet. Those most worthy of respect would be placed in the highest central position. Once the money was paid, a notation about where the placard had been placed was sent to the family and marked in a book. Then any visiting family could easily locate their deceased relative's name.

The shelves used to be filled with placards, but today the names are gone, removed when the government accepted the house. Now incense holders and protective porcelain dog sculptures sitting on altars in front of the bleachers are all that remains of the honors paid to past Chen family members. The records, however, still remain, and an example can be seen in the display on the west wall. It's a photograph copy of a small portion of one of the three bleachers.

"You can try to find if your family members are here," Chilli says as she bends in to look at it closely. She shakes her head at the tiny handwriting, "It's too small." Larger writing fills the ceiling-high wooden plaques with phrases painted in gilt to inspire the family. They hang from the round column supports of the room. Chilli tries to read the notes meant to inspire generations of Chen. "It's hard," she admits, "because they are all in the old style of writing." She says they tell the family to stand and work together. All Chen are Chen.

East of the ancestral hall is a small exhibit hall with dim lights. Raw silk production and woven silk fabrics were a major export in the 1800's, but the true art is found in the embroidery practiced in the region. On display in this small room is the rotating exhibit of embroidered silks. In the West, cotton and wool embroidery floss are the norm. Those threads are thick and make it difficult to produce highly detailed work. In China, hair-thin colored silk threads have been in production and use for centuries[28].

Each art piece in the room appears like a painting and shimmers in the light when the viewer moves. Visitors sway side to side to make the light dance off the wings of a crane that appears ready to launch itself into the room. Such creatures are made from threads sewn into patterns, and each square meter can take months or years to complete[29]. Kay says they are really beautiful but admits that embroidery like this takes too much patience for her to try.

Other galleries throughout the house include the fan gallery which explains the history and traditional production of two styles of palm fan. "They're from the modern time. We have one in our center. This one works really well,...but I like AC," says Kay as she looks at the collection. "I'd like to take the little heart-shaped one," she admits. "It's really pretty." It, like many of the modern pieces here, is for sale.

Regional artists are encouraged to produce and sell in the Chen house as a way to continue old traditions and encourage understanding of the folk arts of the south[30]. Samples and examples of regional arts displayed in the house are for sale somewhere on the grounds, including the famed inside-the-bottle painting pieces. An artist, usually in-house, uses extremely precise painting tools to paint on the inside of a small-mouthed snuff bottle or other glass container.

Across the courtyard from the fans is a hands-on gallery that allows visitors to try a local craft. The most common take-away art is the knot tying activity. Guests can practice tying the never-ending decorative red-cord knots which are meant to bring good luck. Picture directions in Chinese and English are set on the table and an aide is willing to give hands-on help to those who need a little extra guidance.

Ivory and bone carvings are also found in the house, but buyer beware of the ivory. "I appreciate the artwork, but I don't like this behavior. You're killing an elephant, technically. So I'm against it," says Kay. Though this is a legal seller of carved ivory, it is extremely difficult to export and import to other countries even with the correct documents. The bone carvings, usually from cow or camel leg bones, are easier to ship, look just as pretty and come from more sustainable sources. A video in the ivory shop shows how these carvings are assembled using a series of pegs, which allows the carver some breathing room if a mistake is made. A damaged section can be unplugged and started again without having ruined the entire piece[31].

Though it is beautiful, this is not the first ancestral hall built by the Chen; that was built in the countryside before it was legal to build ancestor halls in the city. City officials were afraid of house parties and political up-risings, but near the end of the 1700's these restrictions were removed[32]. The original Chen family home was demolished when the current hall was built.

Chen Clan Academy may not be in use as a university dorm today, but it still seeks to offer an education and not just to members of the Chen family. The interior of the house, with its courtyards filled with trees and light gray stone, is several degrees cooler than the bustling city of Guangzhou on the other side of the walls. Visitors are encouraged to take advantage of this relaxing, cool architectural treasure.

Mrs. John Henry Gray to her mother excerpted from her book *Fourteen Months in Canton* published in 1880 and now in the public domain.

Letter VI -

Canton, April 28th, 1877
My dear Mother,

I have been very fortunate since I last wrote you, in being able to see a funeral ceremony in one of the houses belonging to a Chinese gentleman. He is a friend of Henry's, and as we saw the usual emblems of mourning at the door of the house, Henry took me in, glad of the opportunity of showing me the ceremony, which he knew would then be going on.

We entered a large hall, at the end of which stood the coffin of the deceased, who proved to be an aunt of the master of the house. In front of it an altar had been placed, on which offerings of various kinds, candles, and incense burners were arranged. A large coloured portrait of the deceased lady hung on the wall behind. By the side of the altar life-size figures made in paper, representing attendants, were placed; various paper representations, such as sedan chairs of ordinary size, fans, dresses, and boxes, were placed about the hall, ready to be burnt as offerings. These superstitious people believe that by the action of fire the spirit of the thing represented passes into Elysium, and is then at the service of the soul of the deceased.

Many coloured banners presented by friends of the family, containing words complimentary to the deceased, covered the walls. A pretty young lady now came forward from the interior of the house, dressed in plain cotton mourning garments. The Chinese etiquette is most strict on this point, no silk garments and no rouge (which ordinarily is worn to the greatest degree by the ladies) is allowed during the prescribed period of mourning. The young lady was a daughter-in-law of the deceased.

It is difficult to convey to your mind the number of people contained in a Chinese gentleman's house; a whole clan lives together, each male member of the clan bringing his bride home to his ancestral house. The young lady and her sister, who had joined her – both small-footed women – now put on white sackcloth cloaks and hoods, the latter completely covering their faces, and began, after prostrating themselves, to wail the dead.

It was a curious sight to see these two, who had up to the moment of covering themselves with the mourning cloaks, laughed and chatted with one another, suddenly throw themselves on the ground and howl and moan, their heads swaying about to the cadence of their wailing. One felt the whole scene was unreal, merely a necessary piece of ceremonial. The husband of the young lady who first came in, a fine young man also dressed in white, with a pipe in his mouth, walked up and down, and acted as master of the ceremonies.

After the two ladies had wailed piteously to all appearance for five minutes, the young man gave the signal for them to cease. They rose immediately and at once took off their mourning outer garb.

We went into a very pretty, quaint garden at the back of the house, in which was the invariable pond with a bridge over it. We now left the house and went on to the temple, called by the Chinese, "Ten Thousand Years Palace," but known to Europeans by the name of the Emperor's Temple.

We passed through a massive granite arch, and saw the

lofty roof of the temple covered with yellow tiles, which denotes that it is a State endowment. We then went through two courtyards into a quadrangle enclosed by cloisters. Immediately opposite the large entrance gates stands the great shrine, containing the tablet of the emperor.

In the centre of the paved pathway, and also on the steps leading immediately to the shrine, I saw two or three figures of dragons, and a representation of the sun engraved on the stone pavement. No person, it is supposed, will be sacrilegious enough to tread, on these sacred emblems, and therefore no one will dare to walk straight towards the throne of majesty, on which the imperial tablet rests.

The shrine is enclosed by red-stained walls, and the roof is covered by yellow tiles. On entering the shrine we saw a facsimile of the dragon throne at Pekin [Beijing]. It is most elaborately carved and gilded, and is approached by nine steps. The imperial tablet is in red, on which in letters of gold is the following inscription, "May the Emperor reign ten thousand years, ten thousand times ten thousand years."

An alter stands in front of the throne, on each side of which are arranged the insignia of royalty. At the end of the second quadrangle of this temple stands a shrine similar to the one we had just left, which is erected in honour of the empress. In it is a tablet bearing this inscription, "May the Empress live one thousand years, one thousand times one thousand years."

All the mandarins, both civil and military, worship in this temple on the first day of the year, and on the birthdays of the emperor and empress. Here they prostrate themselves and weep when an emperor or empress dies. All officials who may-have occasion to pass this temple must alight from their horses, or sedan chairs, and walk past its gates as a mark of reverence to their imperial majesties.

I was much amused at seeing innumerable cakes of

white wax which were lying on the floor of the second shrine; some hundreds of these cakes looking like white cheeses were there. It is a costly gift annually presented by the wax merchants of Canton to the emperor. One hundred and ten piculs constitute the quantity, and each picul was, Henry says, in 1873, worth eighty dollars [approximately $1,568 USD in 2014 making the total value $172,480 USD[33]].

This insect wax comes from the province of Szechuan, but when it arrives at Canton it is not quite white. Therefore the cakes are broken up into little pieces, placed in sieves, standing on white metal vessels. They are placed in caldrons of boiling water, and the pieces of wax as they melt fall through the sieves into these vessels. When congealed, the wax is made into cakes and exposed to the sun. It certainly was dazzlingly white when we saw it ready for packing.

On our way to this temple we visited a large hall belonging to the Tea Guild. The Guild of the Green Tea Merchants. In its garden, which I found most interesting, is the original quaint bridge and scenery, from which the willow pattern (or rather that part of it which is not mythological) was taken. The truth was, that a young lady eloped with a neighbour from this garden. The angry father and gardener are represented in the willow pattern on this bridge pursuing the runaway couple.

No Chinese story, however, would be considered interesting without a dash of the marvelous, and therefore they proceed to say that, as the angry father was in the act of catching the runaway couple, the goddess of marriage interposed, and metamorphosed them into a pair of turtle doves. This episode, Henry says, is a favourite subject on the Chinese stage.

I very much admired the curious small gateways and windows I saw in this garden; some were in the form of leaves and others in the form of fruits and flowers. After leaving this guild we went over a lacquer-ware factory, and watched the different processes of painting, colouring, etc.

I have forgotten to tell you of one incident of our day's excursion. Before we reached the imperial temple. We arrived at a small turning, as it appeared to be, and Henry came to my chair and asked me to alight. I walked with him on to a narrow, long strip of ground, on which various pieces of pottery were lying about. Its name, from the supposed similarity of shape, is Horse's Head. When asked to guess where I was, I failed to give an answer. I was then told I was standing on the execution ground.

Before I knew this, however, a nice-looking young man came forward from one of the small neighbouring houses, where his wife, child, and mother were standing on the doorstep. Imagine my amazement when Henry told me this was one of the four executioners employed by the authorities. When asked how many heads had fallen to his sword already, he replied one hundred and seventy, and said that on the day following there was to be an execution on a large scale, in which he hoped to have a share.

We heard that forty pirates were to be decapitated. Our friend, who was with us, arranged at once to be present. I saw the crosses on which the men are tied who are condemned to be strangled, or to be cut into pieces, also some large earthenware vessels containing the heads of several malefactors who had been decapitated a few days previous to our visit. I trust that I may never meet a procession on its way to this place teeming with horrors.

The unfortunate criminals are pinioned tightly, are then placed in baskets, and superscriptions, fastened to strips of bamboo, are placed behind their necks, stating their names, their crimes, and their punishments; in this way they are carried to the execution ground. After all I had heard of the wholesale executions in China, the smallness of the ground, and its unprepared state when we visited it, struck me very much.

On quitting this field of blood, we passed through the street called Wing-Ts'ing-Kai, celebrated as the place where the French put to death ninety-six persons, men, women, and children, when the city was occupied by the armies of Great Britain and France. This was to avenge the death of a cook from a French man-of-war, who had been assassinated by some Chinese in a provision shop in this street.

We proceeded from the lacquer-ware factory (where I broke off from my narrative) to the Examination Hall, a place used once in three years for the examination of those who have already taken their B.A. degree, but who are anxious to obtain the higher degree of Kue-Yan, or M.A. The number is very great of those who assemble in this hall for this purpose, frequently exceeding 12,000 or 13,000. Out of this large number of candidates possibly not more than 120 can obtain the degree, as the number is limited by law in each province. It seems to correspond to the patient nature of a Chinese, that a man should try again and again for his degree under such difficult circumstances.

The hall consists of a large quadrangle; branching from each side of it are several long rows or streets of cells, each cell being five feet six inches in length, and not more than three feet eight inches wide. They are open in front; each cell is provided, during the examination, with a bed, which simply consists of seven or eight narrow deal boards. Some of these boards removed from their place by day serve the candidate for a table, and those remaining in their grooves are used by him as a seat. These streets of cells are named by characters from the "One Thousand Character Classic" and each cell is numbered, so the examiners have no difficulty in summoning any particular candidate from his cell.

In the centre of the quadrangle stands a pavilion, made in the form of a triple gateway, to which the name of Watch Tower is applied. The two examiners for each province are despatched from Pekin and are received in the provincial capitals with great honours. The candidates enter the hall according to their counties (at least those who can get in, for the crush is so great that some do not succeed in pushing in until a late hour), at the early hour of four A.M., and have to answer to their names at the second and also the third gates of the hall.

Before they enter the latter gate they are provided with sheets of paper on which to write essays and poems. The candidates have previously paid for their paper at the temple of Kwan-tai, the god of war. At the third gate of the Examination Hall they are searched, to ascertain whether they have provided themselves with "cribs" in the form of small pocket editions of the classics.

A cook and a waiter are allotted to each ten candidates, and they are pledged to hold no communication with them. During the early part of the examination, the candidates, who vary in age from eighteen to eighty, remain three days in their cells, and are engaged in writing essays and poems. The successful candidate in this first examination go in again for another term of three days, when they have to write five essays from themes selected from the five classics.

Those successful in this second examination have yet to go in for another and final examination, which consists of five papers on any subjects chosen by the examiners. Out of those who have thus passed through three times three days of hard examination only 120, as I have already stated, may be chosen.

I have forgotten to mention that the emperor provides

for each candidate, during his stay in the Examination Hall, the food following: – four taels of pork, four taels of ham, six taels of salt fish, congee water, four moon cakes and a quantity of rice, a preserved egg, and a modicum of pickled vegetables [four taels is 0.33lbs or 151.2g, six taels is 0.5lbs or 226.9g[3]]. Those who obtain their M.A. degree wear a dress peculiar to the degree, and a gilded ornament on the top of their hats, and are invited to dine with the governor of the province, when the examination is over.

They are presented to the chief officials at the banquet, and then are required to perform the kau-tau [a kneeling bow with the head touching the floor] before the imperial tablet. They are afterwards escorted through the streets by their friends. Their names are published throughout the province of which they are natives. The last act of the scene is a douceur given by the newly made Masters of Arts to the examiners.

I am afraid I shall weary you with our long day's proceedings. As our friend was with us we were most anxious for him to see all that was possible for him to see during this visit. So, weary as we began to feel, we went on to the "City of the Dead," one of the strangest and most unique places I have ever visited. The two gentlemen were on foot all day. I was in a chair, as I could not do such a day's sightseeing with the additional fatigue of walking long distances.

The "City of the Dead" (so foreigners style these places containing the dead) was at some distance from the Examination Hall and very far from Shameen. It is very difficult to convey to you any idea of this strange, silent city laid out in streets, and on each side of which are rows of small one-storied houses built in stone. I think the only simile I can draw is that of rows of small almshouses.

Imagine the death-like stillness that prevails in this place, where each house is occupied only by the dead. In most cases the room containing the large wooden coffin is divided into two. The first division contains an altar, which has in many cases a light burning over it, and effigies in paper, life size, or nearly so, of male and female attendants, standing by it. There are paper flowers often on the altar; the decorations vary much, according to the rank of the deceased. I saw, in some cases, outside the doors red boards and insignia of rank.

In the middle of the inner division of the room is the large uncovered coffin with the foot of it towards the door. On entering one of these houses of the dead, our friend inadvertently touched one of the paper effigies, which represented a female attendant; she fell into our friend's arms and her neck became dislocated. We could not forbear a smile even in these grim surroundings.

As all cannot afford to pay a sufficient sum for their relations to have a room to themselves in this temporary resting-place, you see four of more coffins in some of the rooms. In one large room I noticed as many as twelve coffins. The doors of the houses are folding doors and can be pushed open easily. We entered many of them, as we passed down street after street. This large city of the dead has 194 houses in it.

The dead only remain here for a time. The relations consult the geomancers as to a lucky spot for interment, and sometimes these soothsayers take a long time before they give an answer. Whilst therefore the relations wait to be assured of a lucky spot for burying their lost ones (a point much thought of by the Chinese, who are most superstitiously anxious to avoid all cause of offence towards the dead), they place them in these receptacles, and pay so much a month for the resting-place.

Sometimes a delay in interment must take place in the case of those who die at a distance from their homes. It is imperatively necessary for a man to be gathered to his own after death, for the purpose of ancestral worship; should he be buried away from home, his spirit, unhappy and dissatisfied at being deprived of the homage of his descendants, might rove about seeking to injure the living to the utmost of its power.

At the entrance of this City of the Dead is a very large piece of water surrounded by trees, inhabited by hundreds and hundreds of storks. These birds are considered sacred in China. The somber water with its deep shades, and these birds uttering their dismal note, form a fitting entrance to a place devoted to such a purpose as this City of the Dead. The only living beings here are a few Buddhist monks, whose duty it is to receive the dead who are brought here, and to pray for the repose of their souls.

One is startled, to see a white cock run out of one or other of these houses of the dead; but I learned from Henry that this proceeds also from a gross superstition. The white cock is supposed, to attract the soul of the dead by its crowing, and thus prevent the spirit wandering away from the body. As I have previously observed, the Chinese believe that each human body is animated by three souls; the first of which is supposed to remain with a tablet bearing the name of the deceased, placed in the ancestral temple; the second to remain with the corpse; and the third to go to Elysium.

My chair coolies seemed to be much relieved when it was suggested that we should return home by boat. As my two companions had walked and stood about for many hours, they did not feel equal to the five miles' walk home, so we made our way to the banks of the river, hired a sampan, and after very slow progress, in consequence of the strong tide being against us, arrived home after eight o'clock p.m., tired and more than ready for our dinner.

Chapter 2 – Guangdong Museum

Guangdong Museum

How to get there: Take metro Line 3 or Line 5 to Zhujiang New Town stop exit B2. Cross the road and park.
Or
Take the APM line to the Opera House stop then walk south through the park.

How much: Free with passport

How long: 2 - 4 hours

    Guangdong Museum is a puzzle, or at least it looks like an ancient puzzle box, a 3D Tetris game. The museum was built to replace the older National First-level Museum, the first of its kind in China, and to house a collection of more than 167,000 pieces. The doors were opened on May 18th, 2010[1]. "You can see something about science, history, culture. Something about Cantonese," says April, a university student studying visual communication. Her hair is tied back away from her oval face and black glasses on this cool autumn day.
    On weekends and holidays the lines can get long, but not during the week. Visitors stroll up the long embankment-sided walkway towards the square building. At the top of the

sloped walk is the entrance where workers punch tickets and usher guests into the central hall. The air conditioning is on, so April doesn't remove her zippered red and white sweater. The space is dimly lit from the skylights four stories above increasing the sense of coolness in the cavernous space.

Built as a box, the hall echoes with noise from the floors above. Cement and metal do little to muffle the cacophony. April spends a few moments looking up at the museum's central space before moving on. A series of display boxes with collection pieces are inset in the floor framing the central stage area. Visitors pass it by as they head towards the shallow wooden stairs that lead to the second floor.

The first and second floors are home to the bookshop and offices but not the collections[2]. Guests continue to the third floor. That floor is divided into two halves: upper and lower. The museum encourages visitors to start their tour on the lower floor which houses the three temporary exhibition halls, the Duan inkstone permanent display and the woodcarving hall. Only two of the temporary exhibits are in use at any given time. One showcases a Chinese cultural display while the other brings foreign cultures to China.

April wanders through the temporary tea display. Looking at a display of leaves she admits, "I'm not a professional, so I really don't know what name they are." To her tea is just tea, and she doesn't drink very much of it. Her mother tells her it will give her a cold, but she's an exception in China. Tiny cups and delicate service pieces on display show the importance of tea here. It's served hot or cold, winter or summer. Tea is used for cleaning utensils at the restaurant table and welcoming a guest. However, many of the delicate pieces on display here were produced for trade with the West, especial the British markets[3].

Britain's love for tea, which blossomed in the 1770's,

was world changing. Proto-Americans used tea to display their anger over tax monopolies at Boston Harbor in 1773. The Opium Wars were about the British creating a drug war because of their fear of drinking themselves into bankruptcy[4]. But British feelings for tea don't come close to the Chinese usage of it in daily life. Loose tea is the preferred choice and tea strainers and tea balls are common shop items.

The exhibit halls are quieter than the central area. Leaving one exhibit, guests flow easily towards the next. This month the foreign culture exhibit features African tribal carvings and masks. April giggles as one little boy points to an anatomically correct male carving. His mother just shakes her head and nods. Last month, this hall was full of deep-sea creatures and mood lighting. Sharp teeth in the mouths of plastic-encased fish that never saw the sun stared outward. Videos about the submersibles that collected them played. Next month will feature an exhibit on New Zealand jade carvings. The tag line notes that both China and New Zealand have traditional jade cultures[5].

The Duan Inkstone hall is a permanent exhibit of carved stones. The well-lit cases each hold several dark, flat stones smoothed and carved with flowers or animals. Some carry inscriptions carved by their users. "You can make some ink...and use the ink to write. For learning calligraphy," says April. "If you use your finger to touch the inkstone, the feeling is just like the skin of a baby's face." It is this smoothness that made these stones so prized.

Chinese writing has existed for at least four thousand years. Carvings on bones and writing on bamboo dates back to the foundations of northern Chinese culture[6]. In 105 C.E. Cai Lun (alternately spelled Cai Jing Zhong) invented wood-pulp paper[7]. Afterwards, writing and reading spread rapidly and a literary boom took place across China. The interest in writing created a need for pens and inkstones of high quality. A solid ink stick is ground on the stone and water is added to create a reservoir of liquid ink into which a horsehair brush is dipped. The Duan stone (named after the ancient Duanzhou city now Zhaoqing city) was notable for, "getting more ink without damaging brush."[8][9]

Duan stones became one of, "the Four Famous Inkstones." The stones are cut from caves in Fuke Mountain and are difficult to quarry because of their location. They range from dark green to purple which appears black. Relief, intaglio, altorelievo and openwork carving styles are common and often more than one is used to achieve a beautiful inkstone[10].

Tang dynasty scholars (618-907) favored a dustpan style stone while Song (960-1279) writers chose a flat, rectangular style. Both styles can be found in the displays. In the late Qing dynasty (1644-1911) a carver named Guo Lanxiang, famous for his work for the royal family, was presented with three first-class stones. Using the natural variations in color in the stone he produced the "Three Famous Inkstones of Guangdong." One of these, titled "Inkstone with the Design of Macaque Holding Peach" or "The Monkey King inkstone" is considered one of the museum's treasures[11]. Modern calligraphers still use inkstones, though production of Duan stones has fallen off. "A lot of students in China learn...calligraphy when they are young," says April.

Visitors should save the Chaozhou Woodcarving art exhibition on this floor for last because it leads to the upper third floor. Through the gateway, designed to look like a house's front door, guests see the twelve tall, dark wood panels crafted as a present for a gentleman who lived a long life. "There's some poor people and rich people in it. I can see some rivers and mountains...It's like a peaceful picture, but not that plain. I like the color," says April. The broad border is covered in gilt flowers and branches. Stories and expressions of hopes for longevity entwine throughout the boarder. The interior space features scenes of daily life. "It's a big, wooden birthday card," says April.

Left of the door is a display explaining how wood carving is accomplished. An artist draws the design onto a solid piece of wood. Traditionally, an apprentice chiseled out the rough design. A journeyman or the master finished the delicate work and the master applied the gilt. Only masters were allowed to do the final step – no one else was trusted enough to handle the gold. This style of work came from eastern Guangdong in Chaozhou Prefecture[12][13][14].

Woodcarvings like this usually fall into three categories: architectural decoration, ritual utensils and furniture. The massive gilt-covered shrine at the end of the room is a ritual utensil. At 10 ft. 7 in. (3.28m) it is one of the largest and finest shrines of this style in China. Tablets, inscribed with ancestors' names, were placed inside during religious events and festivals and carried through the city[15][16].

The openwork decorations, in which figures are made 3D by cutting from the outside towards the interior of a single wood block, were usually for decorative effect around the home, falling loosely into the furniture category. "Wooden Crab Cage," made by local master carver Zhang Jianxuan and his apprentice Chen Shunqiang is an example and features ten tiny carved crabs around a wicker-like crab pot. It was the bronze place winner in the Art Fair of the World Youth Festival in Moscow in 1957[17][18].

Visitors are guided towards a faux-house laid-out in the traditional Qing dynasty (1644-1911) style. Carved furniture pieces from the collection fill the rooms. A flat wooden bed sits in the center of the living room. "People owned this kind of bed to sit and chat with friends," April says. "It comes to the end of the Qing dynasty a lot of people smoked drugs laying on it," she admits with a sad tone. The furniture tells the story of the wood carving of the region, but the faux-brick house tells another tale.

Though tiles and bricks were known of and used in Guangzhou as early as the Han period (206 B.C.E – 220 C.E), it was not common practice due to the cost[19]. The gazetteer of Suixi county reported at the time, "The houses are crude. Located by the sea, much wind and moist earth. Where there is much wind, houses wobble; where the earth is moist, [wood] easily rots." Han houses were generally made from bamboo which rotted and caught fire easily. Fires in 1565 and 1566, which killed hundreds in minutes, prompted Lin Dachun of Wuzhou (a province bordering Guangdong) to put one thousand men to work making bricks which were given to the poor[6]. The green tiles and brick walls of the Guangdong communities became the norm. The cities and towns became a series of narrow passages between solidly built brick houses by the Qing period.

The false home guides visitors around its interior to an exterior facade and more gallery displays. The stairs to the upper third floor appear to the left, while display cases of gilt-encrusted wood encourage more discovery to the right. The golden food container box, used to present offerings to the gods and ancestors is here, surrounded by other glittering pieces[20][21]. One group of visitors is standing around a docent telling a joke about a piece in the display. They laugh and lean in to take pictures. April takes the stairs, skipping the joke. A glance back reveals a painted town scene behind the faux-house.

The upper third floor contains the Exhibition of Pottery and Porcelain through the Dynasties. The first room continues

Guangzhou – Heart of the South

the wood work with another wooden "birthday card," but soon the porcelain takes over. The section on the right is filled with statues and platters painted with colors and detailed scenes of men and women, flowers and animals. Many pieces fit traditional Chinese desires and Western ideals. In a corner stands a rough cast group of unglazed sculptures. They depict a pottery kiln and creation area during the height of the Western craze[22].

"B.C. something to Ming and Qing dynasty. It covers a lot of different styles of pottery. Some pottery is containers and some is just for putting there and showing their reach....It just shows that they are rich," says April. She is strolling through the long gallery, broken into smaller sections by half walls. Pieces of the famous blue-and-white glazeware sit in one case.

The blue-and-white style first appeared in China during the Yuan dynasty (1279-1368). The "Pear-shaped Vase with Flaring Lip and the Design of Figures," is a treasure of the museum and one of approximately three hundred pieces in the world from this period[23]. On the vase, tiny men point forward as they appear to walk around the base. By the 1700's it was so popular in Europe that Dutch merchants began producing delftware, a white-and-blue copy, to capitalize on the craze[24].

Tri-color glazeware with its dripped paint effect, created in the Kangxi period of the Qing dynasty (1644-1911), was the most commonly sold to traders[25]. A Tang dynasty (618-907 C.E.) tri-color statue with a tall horn protruding from the brow of an angry face leers at visitors through the glass. An original of the popular tri-colored horse stands chest forward in another case. The majority of the pieces on display are plates and cups. One plate tells of life in the emperor's court. A yellow dragon floats in the center of a tiny plate marking it for the highest ranking women in the emperor's house, lower status women had to make due with green dragons[26].

Pottery usage was an everyday event in many cultures and household items make an appearance throughout the displays. April notices an ancient chamber pot in one case, "It looks like it's a water container, but I can see it's a toilet." Toy figures of cats are ready to pounce out of their displays, Buddhas bless visitors and farmhouses care for the souls of the dead[27][28]. Many of these daily items are rough and unglazed. April says that the less detail, the more likely the owner was poor.

Leaving the pottery behind, visitors move up the stairs to the fourth floor and choose between two galleries: the Guangdong Natural Resource hall or the Guangdong History and Culture hall. The Natural Resource hall takes visitors down and out of the museum. The History and Culture gallery focuses on the human side of Guangdong. "Guangzhou, we call the 'Southern door' in China, because it's almost at the southernest point in China and it's an important port," says April after entering the culture-focused hall and examining the timeline on the wall. The hall guides visitors through Guangdong's history from Maba Man's lifetime to present day.

Maba Man lived at least 128,000 years ago and researchers believe he was middle-aged when he died[29]. His remains were found in an archaeological dig site in northern Guangdong. He belongs to the group Homo sapient sapiens (modern humans) and was part of a family or tribe who buried him with grave goods. Forensic anthropologists have created a 3D model of what they think he looked like. His model head and real skull sit in a case with other items found at the site[30][31]. Archaeological digs have increased in the past fifty years, with most sites in the northern parts of Guangdong.

Until the Song dynasty (960-1279), most of the Pearl River delta was submerged or often flooded, making the chances of finding well-preserved archaeological evidence

Guangzhou – Heart of the South

unlikely. Major river flow patterns changed during the Song dynasty. The North River shifted its banks and connected the southern portion of Guangdong with the northern half. Trade increased on this new waterway. People also began to build dikes and reclaim lands from the delta. Evidence of the land reclamation is found in the modern main road. It follows the old division between the "sands" and the dikes because that's where the towns emerged[32].

The museum doesn't linger in the Neolithic, Han or Song dynasties. It rushes forward into direct trade with Europe and the region's connections to maritime trade. By the 1500's Portugal was doing business in Guangzhou and other European nations would soon follow[33]. Scale models of the sailing ships which would crowd into the port grace the wall of the entrance. Half of a Chinese junk, its hull carved open, sits in the middle of the exhibit's first hall. Visitors can walk through the ship and view the storage system for all the goods carried away daily from Guangzhou port. Ye Quan, a Chinese visitor to the city in 1565 wrote:

"In Guangzhou city, all the households, big and small, have a business. Things are cheap. Not only are local products such as copper and tin sent beyond the province and made into utensils...[I]n Guangzhou city, business is done when a profit of 10 to 20 percent is reached. For this reason, merchants gather there. Moreover, there is a foreign market, where goods are stacked in heaps and people bump shoulders. Even small lanes are noisy..."[34]

The paintings on the walls, scenes from Guangzhou, are part of the cultural exchange that occurred due to contact with the West. Using a Western style with traditional Chinese painting techniques, the Chinese export painters captured the scenery and customs of Guangdong in the 18th and 19th centuries. Several pieces by famed artist Youqua hang here.

They are almost photographs of Guangzhou's low profile and open river. His "A Panoramic View of the Waterfront at Canton" painted in 1845 shows the port alive with Chinese junks and Western vessels[35][36][37].

Though Guangzhou benefited financially from the trade agreements, it didn't always maintain good relationships with the traders. Portuguese missionaries were sometimes sent home[38]. Westerners were attacked in the periods leading up to and after the Opium Wars. Locals argued the pros and cons of Western trade for years. Generally, the con side pointed to the sale of contraband goods from ship to ship as a reason to either more strictly control trade or cease altogether. Illegal sales of gunpowder, weapons and eventually opium were the greatest concerns[39]. The museum directly mentions the Opium Wars only briefly in a heavily glossed text printed on a sign at the back of the main hall. There is no mention of how Shamian Island was built to appease European demands for a permanent trade settlement, nor of how they were given the island to keep them separate and safe from the local population[40].

The collection is housed in a series of winding corridors and open galleries that often conceal the next turn. Many visitors' miss entire sections of the collection because they are unaware there is more to see around a hidden corner. One such section depicts the emigration movement from the 1850's to present day. Immigration cards, suitcases and personal knickknacks fill the cases. By the 1870's, a major emigration movement from the Guangdong region was taking place[41][42]. Chinese moved to Malaysia to work in the tin mines, to the USA to build the railroads or act as "camp followers" (laundry services, restaurateurs and prostitutes) or to Cuba to work in the sugar cane fields in conditions close to slavery[43]. This mass migration from the south is why Cantonese is the language in Chinatowns around the world. This side of the hall ends with an overview of the rise of the modern political party and the Japanese occupation of the 1930's and 1940's.

The other half of the hall focuses on minority cultures and celebrations. The prized piece here is a dragon boat. It's 131 ft. long (40m) 3.9 ft. wide (1.18m) and seats eighty people[44][45]. Everyone faces the same direction and paddles in sync with a drummer on the boat. The "Flower Dragon-boat," noted for its brightly painted decorations, won the championship in the Guangzhou International Dragon Boats Invitation Competition in 2004[46]. Dragon Boat Festival is held on the fifth day of the fifth lunar calendar month, usually in late May or June[47].

The holiday purports to honor Qu Yuan, a beloved Chinese poet. In 278 B.C.E. he chose to drown himself rather than see his country occupied by the State of Qin. Locals rushed to find his body and threw zongzi to the fish so they would leave his body alone. Today, races are held around the world and zongzi are eaten as a special holiday food[48]. Traditionally, after Dragon Boat Day the boats have their decorations removed and the wood hulls are sunk into the river mud. This preserves them until they are raised, painted and used again the next year.

The Dragon Boat Festival is most closely associated with the Dan people or "Dragon Households." They are the people, "who lived by the rivers or the sea, who lived on boats, who came and went with the tide, who made their living from fishing, and who would die if they lived ashore," according to one report written in the 900's. These houseboat people were not ethnically different from their land-dwelling counterparts, just too poor to afford land. Tax laws changed in 1700's and "the boat people" began to leave their boats for shore[49]. This trend increased in the 1900's.

The other cultural group highlighted by the museum are

the Hakka. "They speak a different language. It's a little bit similar to Cantonese, but totally different from Mandarin," says April. She is standing in a hall next to a classroom filled with life-size dolls of students and teacher. The recorded voices of Hakka children recite a lesson over the speakers above. Hakka people were originally settled in the north along the coast closest to Taiwan. In 1661, the Ming dynasty was failing and its leaders fled to Taiwan to regroup. The new Qing rulers forced an evacuation of the coast to cut off any aide the Ming leaders might receive from the mainland. The edict was in effect from 1661 to 1669[50][51].

"People led their cows and carried their seed on their shoulder poles, carrying their elderly on their backs and their young in their arms. There was wailing everywhere," wrote an anonymous witness. Bandits, disease and starvation went with them. When they reached the southern cities one author wrote, "They were starved to the bone; it was too painful for words." Those who refused to move were rounded up and executed[52]. These refugees settled outside of the main towns in enclaves and maintained their traditions. Local Guangzhou families still think of the Hakka people as "northern" people, says April.

Museum visitors finish the tour of Chinese culture by strolling through a faux-street built to resemble a neighborhood in the 1930's. This neighborhood is lit for evening. A bicycle leans against an electricity pole, and a covered truck lurks in a dark corner. It feels deserted, as many streets were during the Japanese occupation[53]. April chose not to enter.

The final exhibit of the museum is dedicated to the rocks, plants and animals found in the Guangdong region. The entrance is bordered by a plaster-stone wall with tree branches stretching over the top. "This is some resources of this area," says April as she walks into the hall. The wall guides visitors towards the mineral displays. Plaques explain the seven geographic areas of Guangdong. The first display cases show the local mineral wealth mined in the region[54]. The cases and pieces are educational and well-designed, but April isn't impressed with mining. "Rocks. Red rocks, white rocks, black rocks, gray rocks. A lot of things about rocks," April says as she looks around the displays. Another plaster wall leads to a hall filled with carved and cut semi-precious and precious stones. She bends down to look at a peacock-blue crystal in a lit case and admits that it and some of the others are quite pretty.

The next room is filled with cases of herbs pressed flat under plastic – preserved for guests. The sub-tropical climate of Guangdong is an ideal area for a variety of different herbs, berries and plants to grow. Many are used in traditional Chinese medicine[55][56]. Guangdong functions as an herbal distribution center, continuing the long tradition of trade in internal markets as well as international[57]. April finds one plant and its fruit she recognizes pressed between plastic plates. "We, our Cantonese, always eat [this], especially in summertime. There's a hard brown skin covering it and there's white meat in it which is sweet...It's good for your brain and your skin," she says.

This room appears to be a dead end. An optical illusion conceals the hallway – the walls only appear to connect. A docent is usually standing by to point visitors in the right direction past the central herb display. A wooden walkway begins as visitors enter the taxidermy area. Each tiny habitat area is frozen in time. On an island a stuffed native black bear rears up next to other animals including a glass-eyed pangolin. The small ant-eating mammal looks similar to an armadillo.

Pangolins are fast approaching extinction because of recent human actions. They are, "being eaten out of existence," says a 2014 report from the International Union for Conservation of Nature (IUCN). The recent demand for wild meat in China has grown as newly rich shoppers seek luxury food items[58]. Beijing, Shanghai, Singapore, Hong Kong and Guangzhou are all in the top twenty cities with the most billionaires according to WealthInsight[59]. April would prefer to see these animals alive, and thinks even zoos are, "a place full of sadness."

The walkway winds through a forest landscape and then folds back. It moves guests through a wetland of dusty cranes and stuffed ducks. The wooden walkway ends at displays of stuffed turtles and snakes. Their skeletons hang pinned above them on the wall. Skeletons stand on either side of the hallway which leads to the final gallery.

Visitors step out of the hall at the top of a vast open room stretching two stories deep. Here the skeletons give-way to plaster-casts of aquatic animals "swimming" down from the ceiling on heavy fishing line. A blue whale surrounded by smaller cousins fills the ceiling ocean. April doesn't like fish, but she likes whales, because they are often shown in cartoons.

Following the platform which edges around the room, guests pass several replicas of local aquatic inhabitants. The sea creatures give way to the brachiosaur, whose feet are planted on the floor below. The long-necked dinosaur stretches its skeletal head up so guests can take pictures with it. Visitors use stairs at the back of the hall to descend to the lower exhibit space.

The stairs lead to a corridor with plaques explaining how fossils are made and discovered. The end of the tunnel-like hall puts guests face to fossilized tentacles with the crinoids. The flat, one story tall stone wall display of the "sea lilies" looks like a tangle of lily pad stems attached to feather headdresses. Their family tree can be traced back to the

Guangzhou – Heart of the South

Ordovician geologic period, roughly 485.4 to 443.4 million years ago – millions of years before dinosaurs – and members of the crinoid family are still floating around in the oceans today[60][61]. A turn to the left and the museum's dinosaurs are on display. A small T-rex, a stegosaurus and a few others make up the small collection.

In 2008, scientists uncovered the world's largest collection of dinosaur fossils in a single site. The city of Zhucheng in eastern Shandong province, dubbed "dinosaur city," saw 7,600 fossils recovered from a 980 ft. (299m) long pit. Thirty more sites around Zhucheng are also being excavated. Several new species have been found in these digs. Unfortunately, many specimens are smuggled out of the country and sold abroad[62][63]. The Guangdong museum's collection is typical of local museums which have yet to benefit from these digs. The fossil collection ends with the rise of mammals at the back of the hall.

Though not all the signs are in English that is no reason to stop a visitor from taking a look around. "This museum is not only about old, pretty old culture," says April. She had a good time wandering around and thinks children will really enjoy it. Views of the park and city from the windows stocked with sitting areas are unbeatable. It's a pleasant retreat during the hot summer and rainy winter.

Mrs. John Henry Gray to her mother excerpted from her book *Fourteen Months in Canton* published in 1880 and now in the public domain.

Letter XIX -

Canton, April 23rd, 1877
My dear Mother,

I had neither time nor space to write all I had to say in my last budget, and could not therefore describe to you an amusing interview we had had with some Chinese ladies in our favourite retreat, the Taai-Tung-Koo-tsze monastery. On paying a certain sum of money, ladies are allowed to occupy the chief rooms for a time, and monks, few in number as they are, retire to smaller rooms below.

The object these ladies had, we found, in coming to this monastery, and remaining in it two or three days, was to worship Koon-yam, the goddess of mercy, and to pray to her for the souls of those who, having died, have left no one behind them on earth to pray for them, and are therefore supposed to be flitting about, unappeased and angry, capable of annoying the living in every possible way. This particular worship, with its accompaniments of offerings of paper money, and paper clothes, and the letting off of a great quantity of fire-crackers, is going on in all parts of the city.

These Chinese ladies, seeing us in the garden from their windows, invited us upstairs to pay them a visit. We were spending the day, as we so often do, in our garden lionse, which was perhaps two minutes' walk from the apartments where the ladies were staying. Henry was allowed to go upstairs, and my little friend [Minnie, a young Chinese girl who acts as an interpreter for Mrs. Gray in exchange for

English lessons] accompanied us. They seemed so pleased to see us, made us sit down, and waited upon us, bringing us tea, melon-seeds – which the Chinese ladies most adroitly break open with their front teeth – preserved pineapple, and cake.

These ladies did not belong to the higher rank of society like the Howqua family, but they were gentle and refined in tenor. Two out of the seven had small feet. One of them decorated my hair with natural flowers, which were standing in a saucer to be used for ornamenting their coiffures. They were much amused with the fairness of my arms, comparing them with their own brown arms.

One of the ladies cracked the melon-seeds for me with her teeth (one must put away one's natural prejudices when one moves amongst a strange people), and all were most attentive to me. There is something very winning and unselfish in the way a Chinese lady behaves towards her guest; she does not seem to wonder what we foreigners think of her – her whole manner is as artless and unstudied as that of a child. They always regret that I cannot speak to them, but say, I suppose to console me, that will come "maan-maau".

A strict fast from meat is observed whilst this worship for the souls of the uncared-for departed takes place. Certain boats, only used for religious purposes, are hired at this time by those who are anxious to join in the worship, and priests are hired to chant services for the spirits of the men who have died unwept and unhonoured. These boats are most brilliantly illuminated, when darkness has set in, from stem to stern by multitudes of lanterns, and as they glide down the river they have a fairy-like appearance.

The monotonous chant of the priests sounds most Catholic, and one could fancy it was a Gregorian strain rather than a chant from the lips of heathen monks. The small lanterns are suspended in endless number from the masts and ropes, and the boat is outlined and covered with these bright-coloured lanterns. The effect of one of these boats as it floats by our house is as of a thing of magic, and the reflection in the river is brilliant. The priests throw burning paper clothes and paper money into the river as they recite the prayers for the dead.

These paper clothes and mock money are supposed to become spiritualized by the action of fire, and so to be adapted to the use of the poor, naked, craving ghosts flitting on the surface of the water. A small boat, with a fire burning in it, is rowed in front of the larger one in which the religious worship is going on, to the accompaniment of musical instruments. A gong is beaten at intervals to attract the spirits to the spot.

Several smaller boats, also having fires burning in them, capable of holding one man only, are rowed by the side of the floating temple. The object of these is to show the spirits the spot where the paper clothes and paper money are being thrown into the river for their use. Oil lamps are also placed in small earthenware vessels, and float in the track of the large boat to serve as guides for the spirits. Truly, one exclaims, this is a superstitious people, wedded to their own idolatrous belief and customs!

The weather has become cooler since I last wrote to you, and we have had much rain and high winds. On the 21st, about noon, we suddenly heard a curious sound like that of a large steamer coming up the river. The boat population at once screamed out in fear, and talked loudly, rowing at the same time as hard as they could to the shelter of the river wall. Henry was writing at the table in the dining-room, the windows of which were as usual open to the ground.

In a moment all his papers were blown off the table on to the floor. On looking out from the verandah we saw that the river was agitated into waves, and the wind was rushing madly towards us, making a wide path in the centre of the river. All was confusion. Our servants called out "Typhoon! typhoon!" (which means "large wind! large wind!"), and immediately closed all the windows and the typhoon shutters. The rain came down in torrents, and was driven before the hurricane.

The noise of voices raised to a high pitch of alarm continued to increase as the boats were hurried past our windows to the creeks where the chance of safety was greater. The people vociferated as Chinese only can vociferate when any calamity takes place. We soon heard that an accident had occurred just to the left of our house: a boat had been capsized, and two children, of six and eight years of age, had been washed out of it and drowned. They were picked up by the crew of a gig belonging to one of the steamers, and were placed on the bund close to our house.

A Chinese doctor happened to be on the spot, but he could render no aid, as life was extinct in both children. Family affection is great in China, and the mother of these children was screaming in her grief, wringing her hands, and imploring the doctor to give her back her children. (This assertion may seem strange after my remarks, in a preceding chapter, on infanticide. It is, nevertheless, true, and may be regarded as one of the many incunsistencies which mark the Chinese character.)

This hurricane, and the same applies to all storms of wind, was supposed by the Chinese to be caused by the dragon, which inhabits the Pearl River, turning himself, and twisting his tail out of the water. One of our coolies, an intelligent man, gravely told us that yesterday, at the commencement of the storm of wind, he saw the dragon's tail lifted out of the water, and that a little boat was raised on it. Our old book coolie, however, would not subscribe to this, and when Henry questioned him he said that Chan-ashu (the coolie) might have seen the dragon, but that he believed the big wind came from heaven.

So you see, even here amongst the believers in the combined teaching of Confucius and Buddha, there is a difference in points of faith. The river dragon is supposed to possess the power of keeping in durance vile a limited number of souls, and calling those he desires to him. When a certain number of men are newly drowned, so many souls in proportion become free from the dragon's power, and can ascend from the water. This is one great cause why the Chinese will not help drowning people. They fear, by doing so, they might make the soul angry whose turn it is to escape from the dragon's power, and that, when it has an opportunity, it would do some harm to them.

The river dragon is much feared, and therefore much worshipped, by the population living in boats. We have since heard of other accidents caused by this mighty rush of wind. Two passenger boats, carrying a great number of people, were upset and the passengers drowned. Some houses were blown down, and the inhabitants who were in them were badly injured. It was a mercy we were not on the river at the moment.

We had intended to cross over to Fa-tee to sit in our garden house, and it was arranged that Henry should go first, and Minnie and I were to follow after luncheon. Henry would certainly have been on the river at the moment of the hurricane, if a heavy shower had not preceded it, and prevented him from starting. This is a dangerous and treacherous river, and I am very nervous at times when making excursions on it.

This year especially it has been most unsafe, from the strong currents and overflowing tides. A boat was caught the other day in an eddy close to the city, and went down head foremost. I am very anxious about Henry's weekly journeys to

Whampoa, and it is very late before he gets home to put my fears to rest. It has been two o'clock, and even past that hour, before he has reached Shameen, when the wind and tide have been against him. He starts from Whampoa about half-past nine p.m. He cannot take a nap, as if he were to do so his four boatmen would give in and not attempt to pull with all their remaining strength against the tide.

After the storm came the calm, and we were able to cross the river (I with no feeling of security) and spend the afternoon at Fa-tee. On our return home about seven o'clock, we saw the curious ceremony of burning paper clothes and paper money in a street on the banks of the river. We rowed towards the spot, and went ashore to see what was taking place. Large piles of paper money had been burnt, and along the river's bank in this neighbourhood I saw a row of red candles alight. I suppose there must have been two or three hundred of them. This particular worship for the souls of those who have died in the streets was given by the proprietors of a large warehouse.

Before the warehouse a lone table was placed, and on it was spread a great variety of offerings in fruit and vegetables. These are exposed for a given time, during which the spiritual part is supposed to be accepted by the hungry ghosts. The material part is then taken home and provides a feast for the worshippers. We saw on our way home many of these grand illuminations and burning of paper money and clothes, taking place at intervals along the banks of the river. All this is done in honour of the spirits of the poor, and of those who have none on earth to pray for them. These ceremonies last from the 1st to the 15th day of this seventh month of the Chinese year.

We sit out on the bund immediately opposite our house, or on our verandah, after dinner, as it is too hot to remain indoors. I am lost in admiration of the pretty fire-flies which flit about in all directions, and look like small lanterns in the distance. I enjoy our walks into the city and its suburbs as much as ever. We buy blue china in all parts of the city, and the other day found two good plates in a most curious little shop in the purlieus of the city. I am also anxious to collect some of the beautiful Chinese embroidery in silk. It is most charming in taste and design.

We have a queer little man, a dealer in embroidery, who visits us at times when he has anything he thinks will tempt us. "That work man have come," our boy says to me, and away I go at once to inspect the treasures he has brought, I generally find the queer little man, with a pipe in his mouth, sitting in the library with my husband. He displays what he has with him, and if it should be a grand embroidered coat, the ugly little one-eyed man puts it on, stretching out his arms wide so that we may see the whole pattern on it.

He names his price, generally a high one, and Henry says quietly, "No can, too muchee money." The little man then takes his seat again and puffs at his pipe. After ten minutes' interval at least, he names a rather lower price, but most probably still too high. Sometimes we come to terms; sometimes he departs with all he has brought. Once or twice he has gone to the servants' quarters, and there waited, and after some time has sent one of the boys in to make an offer at a lower price.

A great deal of the beautiful old work comes from the theatres, for they do not adopt the European custom of painting or working for effect at a distance. All is genuine and good, and the costumes and decoration in China must cost each trading guild which gets up a theatrical representation a considerable sum of money. Some of the embroidery now in our possession has been used in theatres. It looks quite fresh, and is very handsome. Some of it is embroidered in gold on scarlet cloth, and part of it is gold embroidery in beautiful scrolls and patterns on a black ground.

I was much amused with our little Chinese friend the other day. He had brought some embroidery for us to see, and displayed it in our drawing-room over the sofa, chairs, etc. We had then just purchased some large black carved wood chairs, two for ourselves, which were place in our drawing-room; and four others, bought for friends, stood in the dining-room. The little man's quick eye saw the new furniture, and within two or three days he brought us six beautiful red chair-back covers and seats, which were embroidered in gold.

These covers and seats are used by the Chinese on fete days, and look so bright and handsome on the black wood furniture. After some discussion we purchased two of these tempting pieces of embroidery. One curious fact in Chinese furniture is the little variety one meets with in it in size and pattern. I begin to know all the devices. The chairs are either small, and so of a size for use at table, etc., or of a large size, with arms, to be used in reception halls. There was therefore no doubt about these chair-covers, which were intended to go tight over the backs and arms of the chairs, being the right size.

Chapter 3 – Museum of the Nanyue King of the Western Han Dynasty

The Museum of the Nanyue King of the Western Han Dynasty

How to get there: Take metro 2 to Yuexiu Park stop exit D. Turn right and follow the road.

How much: 12 RMB

How long: 3 - 5 hours

The history of the Guangdong region is not complete without a look at the Nanyue kingdom. The Museum of the Nanyue King of the Western Han Dynasty takes visitors back in time and shares the treasures found buried with the king and at other archaeological dig sites in the region. The heart of the museum is the tomb of the second Nanyue king around which the museum was built. Jason, a university student preparing to emigrate to New Zealand, is visiting this museum for the first time since he was a child. His teacher brought him when he was in primary school, but he doesn't remember any of the displays he saw. He takes the entrance stairs which rise between Nanyue-style tiger statues leading to the front hall.

The museum was first opened in 1988, and completely renovated in 2010. The new museum takes elements from modern Lingnan architectural style and decorative elements from objects found in the tomb. It won six architecture prizes, both nationally and abroad, and has been given an AAAA-level tourist attraction title. It is listed as a heritage site by the Chinese government and has been under the protection of the state since 1996[1].

The Nanyue kingdom began not long after the end of the Qin dynasty (221-206 B.C.E). A local chieftain of the sino-peoples, Zhao Tuo (alternately spelled Chao T'o), came to power and declared himself king in 203 B.C.E. In 196 he changed his name to Emperor Wu, but was forced to give up the title in 180 after a defeat by the newly strengthened Han dynasty. He was allowed to maintain his status, however, and rule over the territory as a vassal king to the Han[2][3]. The tomb visitors see was built for the second king, Zhou Mo (r.133-122 B.C.E.) the grandson of Zhao Tuo. Though not technically allowed to call himself emperor, seals found in the tomb with him bear this title, and others are inscribed with his name and helped to identify the body[4].

The museum is housed in three buildings: the specialized exhibition hall, the tomb itself, and an exhibition building for the unearthed relics of the tomb. The entrance is through the specialized exhibition hall. It's a terra-cotta red, three-story square building that leads visitors up the hill into which the king's tomb was dug. Each floor displays relics found in archaeological dig sites around Guangdong[5]. The artifacts tell the story of the southern people leading up to the Nanyue king's rule. The second floor also showcases a collection of ceramic pillows.

The first floor houses the information desk and the museum store. The exhibit begins on the next floor with a copy of the Maba Man headcast. "He looks handsome," Jason says looking at the moustached head. The light is dim here and voices are hushed. Jason says that he can't read the information cards explaining what he's seeing. The Chinese phrasing is confusing and not every display has an English translation. A carved wooden baby, used as a drain spout decoration fills one display. It is creepy says Jason, "like a zombie."

Pottery shards have been pieced back together in one case, while small pottery farm houses and toy-sized pottery people fill another room. When Jason sees one of the little pottery men with slant painted eyes he says, "He has tiny eyes, mine are bigger." He jokes about the Chinese stereotype. These little farms and farmers were common grave goods and sometimes were used as urns for cremated bodies in the region[6]. Similar items were found in the tomb. "They were to follow the emperor...to serve him in Hell," says Jason.

The history of Guangdong may start with Maba Man and his tribe of hunter-gatherers, but the history of Guangdong as China starts with the invasion of the Qin empire in 221 B.C.E. Before this time, the people of the region were closer, ethnically and culturally, to the Thai-Malay people. The Ling mountain range provided a natural barrier between north and south. This changed when the First Emperor, Wu, of Great Wall and terra-cotta warrior fame, decided to expand his territory in every possible direction. The Ling Mountains would not be allowed to stand in the way of the Emperor's will[7][8].

To bring the Baiyue – the name given to the southern peoples by the northern Chinese at this time – into the empire, one of the greatest and most enduring engineering feats was begun. The Ling-ch'ü, or "magic transport", is a three-mile canal that crosses the mountains. Hand dug by workers facing yellow fever and malaria, it joined the headwaters of a southern Yangtze River tributary to a northern tributary of the West River, connecting the northern regions with the southern. The canal allowed supplies to flow uninterrupted to the

47

military forces of Qin as they marched into the new territory. The canal and waterway systems were continued, and today extend 1,242 miles (2,000km). This system is still in use and ties food and material production in central China to ports on the coast[9][10][11].

What the Qin army found when they entered the southern region was a small native population and fertile land. The emperor ordered colonization and had 30,000 ethnically Chinese families move to the region in 219 B.C.E. For their migration they were exempted from labor services for twelve years. With them came groups of convicts and other disfavored people to work as cheap labor. More deportees would be sent to the Guangdong region in 213[12]. So began the Sino-ization or "Chineseing" of southern China. Emperor Wu died and his empire crumbled in only a few years. The southern region was once again separated from the north politically, but the process of acculturation had begun.

Jason and several small groups of visitors move through the exhibit. The design of the rooms guides guests slowly forward in time to the Nanyue kingdom's rise to power then ushers them up the stairs to the doors leading out to the tomb. Covered walkways are placed around the outside edges of the grass covered hilltop. A glass pyramid sits in the center of the grassy square and protects the tomb below from the weather and other possible damage. Apartment buildings rise next to the museum and look into the little courtyard. "Chinese believe that if you live nearby a tomb you'll get unlucky. At midnight you'll see a ghost. But this place is peaceful. It's unexpected," says Jason. Birds hop around on the neatly trimmed grass. One young boy with his parents talks about how cool seeing the dead people will be as they walk towards the tomb.

The tomb itself is in a stone-lined pit inside the

pyramid. A flight of wooden stairs allows visitors to enter and leave. The tomb is several rooms lined with carved stone slabs built into the hill. Once the body of the second king of Nanyue was inside, it was sealed. Then it was forgotten about until being discovered by construction workers in 1983. When it was found archaeologists determined that the stones had cracked over the years and allowed water to seep in. The water had damaged the bodies and any natural fibers, but many of the grave goods were intact[13].

After descending the stair into the first chamber room, visitors find money crumpled and left on the stone ledges around them. This isn't donation money for the museum; it's there for the ghosts. Visitors are encouraged not to touch it. "When they move the body to another place, during the path they leave coins...that is for the little ghost. Give the little ghost money. 'Ok, back off'," explains Jason. The bodies of this tomb, or the fragments of the bodies, have been moved to the relic exhibition hall[14].

Jason is 5 ft. 10 in. (1.78m) and has to duck through the doorways and be careful of the low ceilings built for people much shorter. The tomb has seven rooms and contained sixteen bodies. The central chamber is the main coffin chamber where the king, in his jade suit, was entombed. Based on the other bodies' accessories and seals, the others were four concubines (Lady Right, Lady Left, Lady Tai, and Lady Bu), a court official, and ten servants including one found in the chamber with the musical instruments who might have been a musician. Only the remains of Lady Left and the king were found in large enough fragments to preserve. The rest were destroyed by water and time. The concubines and servants were sacrificed to travel with the king into the afterlife and care for him there[15][16]. It was not uncommon for favored concubines to be put to death when the emperor or king they served passed on. New kings didn't want to father children with the mistress of the old king, it seems.

"The emperor's toys. They used to entertain in this room," says Jason as he crouches down in the tiny west room. He stretches out his hands in all directions and touches the walls on both sides easily. This room is where objects for rituals, weapons, ornaments for horses and carriages and things for daily use were stored. The gold-inlay tiger-tally was found here during the dig. It is the basis for the tiger sculptures at the front entrance. The tiger-tally functioned as a royal pass, and the inscription carries instructions for the receiver[17]. "That tiger was a passport in ancient China. It's really interesting, but I think that the tiger is really heavy. Who would carry a heavy passport to walk around China?" Jason asks.

Other rooms included the store room, where more than one hundred bronze and iron cooking vessels were found along with traces of fruits, fish-bones and other food stores. Officer Tai, the official in charge of food and drink for the royal family – and possibly a relation of Lady Tai the concubine – left several clay seals with his inscription in the tomb. He placed the food in the chamber before the burial and then got out. The east side room was the music store room. Several sets of bronze chime bells, two sets of stone chime bells, zithers and "Liu Bo" chests were discovered near teapots and wine containers in this room. The king apparently enjoyed luxury and entertainment[18][19].

After exploring the tomb, visitors use the same wooden stairs to return to the surface. A metal walkway stretches around the outside of the tomb giving a bird's eye view of the cracked cover stones while leading towards the back exit. Leaving the pyramid, visitors face the main steps leading to the largest of the halls where the treasures unearthed in the tomb are stored and studied. To the right is a circular tower where several cannon are placed. Used as an armament placement during the Opium Wars, it failed to successfully defend the city[20].

The hall's exterior walls feature bas-relief "carvings" based on the decoration found on a bronze vessel during the excavation[21][22]. It was found in a well near the tomb and is thought to be part of the original collection. The vessel illustrates that the native people in the region were not northern Chinese. A warrior in a feather headdress is standing on a crescent-shaped canoe and holding out a human head in one hand. The style of the work might make Western visitors think of the Aztecs rather than the ancient Chinese. These people were the Baiyue, but they had been replaced as the dominant group in the region by the time of the tomb's creation[23].

The exhibition hall is divided into six areas which group the objects found in the tomb together by type. The first area is specifically for those things relating to the body and burial of King Mo. The seals are here. When pressed into hot wax or clay they produce a copy of the seal's face, like a stamp. They were used as a signature[24]. The king had several, the most notable being the solid gold seal[25]. It's almost an inch square (2.5cm^2) and has a dragon curling across the surface. Its body rises from the base to form a loop for a cord so it could be worn like a necklace. The ladies each had seals which marked their high social standing in the court. Other members of the court placed their seals in the tomb, but were not themselves buried there[26].

After the seals, there is a copy of the highly decorated wooden coffin in which the king was buried, of which only the bronze handles survived intact. Small fragments also survived[27]. It was so large it had to be slid into the tomb and the door built after its placement. Around the corner rests the jade body-formed shroud and pictures of the king's remains.

"This body is covered by jade clothes. Actually, that clothes covers everything. I think it protects the body from disease. He doesn't look good...," says Jason as he peers into the case where the jade suit is on display. The suit is made of pale green jade scales tied together with red ribbon. The photo of the body shows the decayed and limited remains of the king when he was unearthed. Some of his teeth and the seed pearls that were stuffed in his pillow are found in a case in the next room[28].

The second section of the exhibition hall is dedicated to the jade pieces found in the tomb. Jade is not easy to carve, having a brittle quality while being one of the hardest stones. It shatters easily when struck, but is very solid[29]. This helped it survive in the tomb. Hundreds of pieces were recovered. The most famous is a circular medallion with a dragon figure in the center and a phoenix surrounding the exterior. A stylized version is used as the museum's trademark and symbol[30][31].

After spending time looking at it Jason is skeptical. "A dragon is a five animal combination. A cow head and a fish and snake's body and an eagle's claws. But no, it has nothing, so I believe it is a leopard," he says. A cartoon video of the dragon and phoenix play on a nearby screen, but he remains unconvinced. He also notices that the English descriptions of the items and the Mandarin descriptions do not give the same information to visitors. English descriptions seem to focus on production while the Mandarin describes the decorative element.

The necklaces found with the concubines are tacked onto boards. The silk cord that held the half-circles and beads of jade together rotted away, and the museum chose not to replace them. Instead, they present the pieces hanging together in the way they think they would have appeared, draped in long strands. Jade jewelry was used as sign of wealth and status within the court, but it also symbolized courtly virtue and offered spiritual protection. The jade examples found in the tomb are noted for their craftsmanship and beauty[32][33].

The turns and half-rooms that guide visitors from one section to another also reduce noise levels to a murmur. Displays aren't crowded together so there is usually a good view of each item. A set of wide stairs at the end of the jewelry exhibit guides visitors down to the basement level, where the tour continues with daily use jade pieces. These items, like cups and bowls, quickly give way to metal weapons. Bronze spears and iron swords indicate that this was the historic tipping point between the bronze and iron ages in southern China[34][35]. The king, as a show of power, was buried with ten iron swords. One iron sword found next to him measures 4 ft. 7.9 in. (1.46m) and is the longest iron sword from the Han dynasty period yet discovered[36]. Other armor and weapons of bronze and iron were found in the west room including a war chariot and horse accessories[37][38].

Across from the weapons is a display of more common daily existence items, including fishing hooks and nets. Jason stops and looks at the remains of shellfish found in the tomb, now sitting in a glass box. Eating shellfish and other foods the northern Chinese found exotic was an everyday event for Lingnan people[39]. Lingnan culture, often noted for its architectural style, also includes the foods found commonly in this region. Lychee fruit, betel nuts, coconuts, and other subtropical fruits, as well as water-based foods like fish, crawdads, and crabs are staples here. "There is an old joke in Guangzhou," says Jason. "Guangzhou people will eat anything with legs, except tables and chairs." Variations on this joke go on to include: anything that swims, except submarines, and anything that flies, except airplanes. He laughs before strolling to the end of the hall.

The stairs at the end of the basement exhibit lead up to the kitchen supplies from the tomb. Three-legged bronze cooking pots of various sizes fill this room's cases. Some are no larger than modern saucepans; others are capable of cooking half a sheep in their vast interiors. A patina-green garlic grater sits on a raised white square[40]. Nearby a bronze square rests on four legs. Its sides stretch up about two inches (5cm) before curving back into the inside of the pan. Jason recognizes it immediately. Portable barbecues haven't changed much in two thousand years. "This is a barbecue, stove, oven. A bronze oven and used to barbecue," he says. He adds, "I don't trust that the Chinese invented the barbecue. Even though, people say China has invented a lot of things..."

The final area of the hall is reserved for music. The display starts with a single jade carving, which stands no more than an inch tall (2.5cm) and is a pale pink color. This tiny dancing girl, with her long sleeves and tiny waistband, is a prized treasure of the collection[41][42]. Next to her is a room-high black box with sets of bells and chimes set in wooden racks and a hologram of a dancing girl, which plays when visitors pass. One group of visitors is startled when the hologram turns on as they pass.

Several sets of bronze bells were found in the tomb. They have no clappers; instead, they sit upright in a wooden frame and the bell-ringer strikes them with a padded hammer. Each set of bells has various sizes to produce a range of musical notes[43]. "I've heard them. They used to play them in the temple, the old temple," says Jason. The stone chimes, which look like enormous ax heads, are suspended from similar racks and struck. The sets hanging here have not been struck since they were placed in the tomb for fear of damaging them[44].

Turning the corner, visitors are faced with a counter selling trinkets based on the items found in the tomb. Dragon earrings and pendant necklaces copy the jade dragon emblem or the pieces worn by the concubines. Keychain fobs and books written about the site wait for visitors to open their wallets. They are priced a bit on the high side says Jason, but they are not found elsewhere in the city. Then it's only a few steps back into the courtyard and tomb lawn.

There is one more exhibit that is not related to the Nanyue king, often left for last or explored first: the exhibition hall of ceramic pillows. "The pillow looks familiar, because my grandma had one. Like this, just like this, and I've tried it before, but it really cut my neck and I always feel a headache...but my grandma, she is used to it so she had no problems," says Jason as he moves through the gallery of more than two hundred of these ceramic head-holders, collected and donated by Mr. Yeung Wing-Tak and his wife[45][46][47]. Some are tiger shaped, others appear to be lily pads, one encourages the sleeper to dream well in a poem painted on its head platform. They vary in date, with the earliest examples from the Jin dynasty (265-420) and the latest from the Yuan (1279-1368), but most of the pillows were crafted during the Song (960-1279) and Tang (618-907) periods[48]. The room feels like a warehouse, and doesn't match the aesthetic created in the other spaces. Visitors rarely linger over the porcelain pillows and their neck-bending promises.

Finished with all the galleries and exhibits, guests head for the door. "I was expecting the whole museum to describe the whole Nanyue tomb, but the museum is not only describing the Nanyue tomb, but also describing the culture," Jason says as he prepares to leave. "I had a good trip, but I'm a little bit tired."

King Mo's reign occurred during the height of the

55

Nanyue kingdom's glory, a glory that wouldn't last. The fifth and final king, Zhao Jiande, (r. 113-111 B.C.E.) was destined to lose the kingdom. During his reign, Nanyue was set to make a change towards an even more pro-Han agreement which would absorb Nanyue more fully into the Han empire. Led by the queen dowager, a northern-born Chinese, plans moved forward towards this alliance. However, her initiative met with opposition from some of the leaders of Nanyue who did not wish to lose power and place Han interests above their own. In 112 B.C.E., Lü Chia and his supporters turned to violence and murdered the queen dowager. The Han government used the murder as a viable excuse for invading the Nanyue region, a land they wanted to gain greater power over due to the trade blossoming in the area. The Han army destroyed the Nanyue vassal state, putting in its place nine commanderies (two of which would later be withdrawn)[49][50][51]. The south was now firmly established as part of China, though it would continue to be Lingnan.

Mrs. John Henry Gray to her mother excerpted from her book *Fourteen Months in Canton* published in 1880 and now in the public domain.

Letter XX -

Canton, August 25th, 1877
My dear Mother,

On the 2nd inst., the state worship on occasion of the emperor's birthday took place. Henry was most anxious for me to go, as he feared that if I did not embrace the present opportunity, another might not offer. Next year the ceremony may take place on a Sunday; or we might be up the country; or something else might prevent me from seeing this worship paid to the emperor's tablet.

As is always the case with special religious services in China, it was held very early in the morning, in fact at break of day, four o'clock A.M. The spirits are supposed to be more active, more inclined to hear petitions, and to be more especially present in the tablets, idols, etc., early in the day. We agreed to be called at two o'clock A.M. on Monday morning, to go down the river in a slipper boat as far as one of the city gates. A chair was to be in readiness for me there, in which I was to go to the Maan-Shau-Kunng, or Ten Thousand Years Palace. It would have been very inconvenient to go all the way in chairs on account of the closed city gates and barricaded streets through which we should have had to pass, but by performing most of the journey by water, we only had one gate to pass through.

We sent a coolie the night before (Sunday) to promise this gatekeeper a kumshaw [a silver coin] if he would get up at two o'clock the following morning, and open the gate for us.

Guangzhou – Heart of the South

Our plans were upset when the morning arrived, as Henry had had a very tedious row home from Whampoa against a strong tide, and did not reach the Chaplaincy until after half-past twelve. It was impossible for him to attempt another journey, he was so thoroughly prostrated by the fatigue and heat, and his heavy day's work. He would not hear of my giving up our proposed excursion, so, to prevent his attempting what I feared would make him really ill, I suggested that he should trust me with our compradore and Chong-Shing, the teacher.

When the rap came at the bedroom door at two o'clock, I must say that I heartily wished the mandarins were not so early in their habits. We started about half-past two, the two men I have mentioned, our old coolie, and I. The four boatmen in the slipper boat were equal to the duty, although they had had such a heavy pull up from Whampoa. All went smoothly. I found my chair waiting at the city gate, and I got into it.

I was much amused by a feature of extreme economy in my guides. They had started from home in their short jackets, and both carried a little parcel done up in a handkerchief. At this gate the parcel was undone and the two men put on their long coats. Although we arrived at the temple soon after three o'clock a.m., many of the inferior mandarins had already assembled and were seated in an outer court. All these ceremonials are attended by the greatest amount of etiquette it is possible to conceive.

Thus the smallest man starts from his yamun at an hour long before the appointed time of the ceremony, and on leaving his residence he sends a messenger to the yamun of the mandarin next higher in rank to himself, to say that he is already on his journey. Number two then starts, knowing that the inferior will have arrived before him at the rendezvous, and be there to rise and receive him in due time. Number two on starting despatches a messenger to number three, and so on, until the greatest man is reached at last.

Each fresh arrival of a higher mandarin already assembled, who advanced towards the entrance of the robing-room in two rows mute and motionless, whilst the bigger man passed through them with slow and majestic gait, looking neither to the right nor left of him, but proceeding to his appointed seat, all the others following in dignified silence. A mandarin of important rank is simply inflated by pride and pomposity. His movements are all regulated by rules of etiquette. Therefore each man of equal rank is a copy of the one model. So exactly to time is the foot encased in its huge black silk boot brought forward, turned to a right angle, and then raised before being placed forward to take a majestic step, that it gives these mandarins the effect of being moved by wires.

No smile is to be seen of their faces, no expression but one of stereotyped stolidity. When a mandarin seats himself on these public occasions all is again by rule. He raises his long silk coat, gradually drops into the chair, puts his feet in the first position with his knees wide apart, and generally places a hand on each knee. When finally adjusted in his chair, he raises his eyes and takes a dignified look about him, not altering a muscle of his face, nor appearing to be struck by anything he sees.

The three most important men present on this occasion were the Viceroy, the Governor and the Tartar General [the Viceroy was the voice of the emperor for all court matters, the Governor handled all tax and legal issues in the province, and the Tartar, or Mongol/Manchu, General controlled the militia], all mandarins of the first order, and each wearing the much coveted pale red button. The Viceroy takes precedence of the Governor and Tartar General, and is the first man in the province. To show his importance, it was fully a quarter of an

Guangzhou – Heart of the South

hour after the Governor had arrived before we heard sounds of his approaching procession.

The temple itself presented a most fairylike appearance, dimly lighted as it now was with an immense number of oil chandeliers and coloured lanterns painted in various devices. The quadrangle immediately before the shrine which, as I told you in a previous letter, contains a fac-simile of the emperor's throne at Pekin with the emperor's tablet resting on it, was lighted with hundreds of small lights. These lights, were placed four in number, in receptacles, on iron rods which hung from the roof of the cloister surrounding the quadrangle. As no mandarin is considered high enough in rank to enter the shrine itself to worship the tablet, it is in the centre of the quadrangle that the ceremony is performed.

I had been immensely interested in all that was going on around me during the hour of delay before the worship began, in watching the mandarins receiving each other – at walking over to the other side of the quadrangle to see the military mandarins. Two of these were of the first rank and sat on a dais at the end of their robing-room, looking as pompous as man can look. There was a great hurrying to and fro of attendants, who swarmed in the quadrangle. The lowest mandarins have twenty, and mandarins of the first rank, one hundred attendants.

Servants brought into the quadrangle large wooden chests, suspended from their shoulders on bamboo poles, containing suits of mourning apparel for the mandarins. This curious custom is observed on the supposition that the Emperor might possibly die whilst the ceremony is taking place, and so provides that in this case the mandarins should go home in mourning garments. Other boxes carried in by servants contained court hats worn by the mandarins only at the time the ceremony is being performed. In other boxes I saw teapots, cups and saucers, pipes, etc.

The mandarins wear their handsome full court dress on this occasion. The skirt is dark blue silk beautifully embroidered in silk and gold thread; a tippet is also worn, which is much ornamented with gold embroidery. The hat, which is the ordinary pointed official hat, is trimmed fully with a deep fringe of red floss silk, and surmounting the apex is that distinguishing mark of rank, the coloured pear-shaped button.

Every official present rose as the clash of musical instruments announced the near approach of the Viceroy. In two or three minutes he arrived, alighted from his State chair, and passed up the centre of the long row of mandarins standing by the entrance of the robing-room, in the centre of which the Governor was waiting to receive him. The two great men chin-chinned each other, and passed up together to the raised dais at the end of the room, and seated themselves simultaneously.

The twelve mandarins varying from the first to the fourth rank took their seats on benches arranged down the sides of the room, where they had already passed the last hour or more smoking and chatting together, when not required to go to the entrance to welcome a higher brother-official. These robing-rooms were open to the quadrangle, so that from where I stood I could see all that passed in them. The court hats, tippets, and skirts were now put on by the mandarins with the assistance of their attendants.

The three great men then walked slowly into the quadrangle, followed by all the mandarins according to their rank. The Viceroy, Governor, and Tartar General placed themselves side by side before the first three kneeling-mats in the centre of the quadrangle, and the other mandarins arranged themselves in order of precedence behind them. A band of musical instruments accompanying them, ceased playing when all had taken their places; and the master of the ceremonies, standing on the biggest step to the right of the shrine, gave the word for the ceremony to commence. It was this: "Advance, kneel, knock the head."

An inferior mandarin first advanced, and after three repeated kau-taus withdrew. He was supposed to make the offerings to the emperor, which were already placed on the altar before the tablet. The voice of the master of the ceremonies was heard a second time, and now the Viceroy, Governor, Tartar General and every mandarin present, solemnly advanced their left feet forward at the same moment, took them back, then advanced their right feet, knelt on both knees, and bending their heads knocked them three times on the ground. All the company of mandarins then rose, rested a minute until the shrill voice of command was again heard, when they all went through the same genuflections. They again rose and for the third time bent the knee and performed the Kau-tau.

When the three times three had been performed, the whole assembly left the quadrangle in regular order, and each mandarin returned to his appointed place. The centre shrine was a blaze of light: large chandeliers lighted it inside, and little lanterns were hung under the broad roof along the facade of the building. The doors were wide open, and the imperial tablet, the object of worship, was thus visible to all. As I have already described it and its inscription, I will not say more about it now.

I was standing the whole time of the ceremony on the granite steps which occupy the centre of the quadrangle, having the Viceroy and Governor immediately on my left, the Tartar General and some mandarins on my right hand. I returned now with my guides, and took up my position in front of the robing-room.

I saw the high officials disrobe, remove their court hats,

and put on their ordinary mandarin hats; they then sat down, tea was handed, and they chatted together. In a short time I heard some steps behind me, and on turning round I saw the procession of the Tartar General and military mandarins, who had left their robing-rooms, and were advancing to salute the Viceroy, Governor, etc. The two latter rose to receive their guests, chin-chinned them, and placed the Tartar General on the dais. You cannot, without seeing it for yourself, fully understand the manner of these officials. It is self-contained, dignified, pompous, intensely quiet, and brimful of etiquette.

You will wonder how the crowds had behaved to me all this time, and how I had been able, the only woman present, to stand amongst them. Well, the truth is that they took no notice of me at all. All had come to see the ceremony, or to wait on their masters, and I escaped with little observation. Our compradore now said to me, "More better you go that side, 'spose you wantchee see also that largee mandarin go." So I got into my chair, and was carried to a quiet spot to wait and see the processions of the different officials as they left the temple.

But first, I have forgotten to say I had a look at an open-air theater, which was temporarily placed in the outer court of the temple, where a play was being performed whilst the religious ceremony was being held in the temple itself. This play represented an emperor bestowing honours and rewards upon his faithful ministers of state.

There were nine actors on the stage. A throne was erected, and an actor, grandly dressed, representing the emperor, was seated on it, and in a high falsetto key was speechifying. No doubt he was giving some excellent advice. The other actors were arranged on each side of this personage, and were moving about in true dignified, pompous, mandarin style.

After waiting in my chair for half an hour, gongs

announced the approach of some of the officials from the temple. Several mandarins passed me in succession, each accompanied by many attendants, varying in number according to the rank of their masters. Then came the chief procession. Words fail me to describe the extraordinary appearance of these cavalcades. At the head of each came men bearing huge lanterns with the titles painted on them of the great man to whom they belonged; then there were ragged boys carrying the insignia of rank, silk flags, and painted boards with titles upon them in raised characters.

Then equerries, who were handsomely dressed in silk robes and mounted on ponies, passed by. The ponies were but poor creatures, very thin, with their bones nearly coming through the skin, the fat riders in their flowing robes looking very caricatures on their sorry brutes. Then came the military; do not picture to yourself European troops when I mention these. Their legs and feet were bare, and they wore red or red and blue tunics and trousers, very shabby in appearance; their hats I cannot describe, except by saying that some of them were in shape like a tall European hat, only these were made in transparent lattice-work of bamboo.

Others wore headdresses still more difficult to describe. They were made of gold tinsel in the shape of crowns; from the sides of the highest part rose two long argus pheasant feathers, more than four feet in length, made longer than nature intended by being mounted on to wire ends. Picture to yourself this costume, this theatrical headgear, the owner in shabby tunic and red trousers just past the knee, bare-legged, and having no shoes.

The whole struck me as like a pantomime, and appeared still more grotesque as daylight now began to appear. You know we have no dawn here; as the sun rises, so day begins. The lanterns were extinguished, and I saw the members of the procession in their true unvarnished light. And now came the Viceroy in his chair of state borne by twelve men.

He sat with arms raised on the shelves beside him, and his head thrown forward. His stolid expression was preserved. The procession was closed by more mandarins on horseback, attendants bearing flags, insignia, etc. I have not yet mentioned my early ramble in the city to any of the European community. I fear they may think me strong-minded; and what is the use of speaking of these things to those who take no interest in the manners and customs of the singular people among whom they dwell?

Chapter 4 – Temples of Yuexiu District

The Temples of Yuexiu District

How to get there: Take metro line 1 to Ximenkou station exit C. Turn right and follow the road.

How much: Guangxiao Temple is 5 RMB, Liurong Temple is 5 RMB, Huaisheng Mosque is free; however only Muslims are allowed to enter, Temple of the Five Immortals is free with passport

How long: Half Day

Yuexiu district is one of the oldest sections of the city and has been its religious heart for centuries, the home of the original Arab trader population and the seat of Buddhism in the region. The temples and monasteries of Guangxiao and Liurong and the Islamic mosque of Huaisheng have watched the city grow from a small center of southern power to a bustling metropolis. The Taoist temple dedicated to the Five Immortals joined them as the City of the Rams tale grew with the city's prosperity.

Emily is spending the day before Chinese New Year, a pleasantly warm spring day, visiting the temples. She's a business woman with a round face and sarcastic wit who has lived in the city her whole life. She's part of a crowd moving up the street filled with flower and incense sellers. Gold colored papers, folded into lucky pyramids grace folding tables placed on the sidewalks. People crowd together at Guangxiao temple to ask for blessings from the Buddha in the coming year. "I think tomorrow will be very crowded," Emily says, and warns that it's likely your clothes will be burnt by careless people waving incense. Though these temples are busiest during holiday times, there are always a few people wandering the open-air courtyards of the temples.

Guangxiao temple's entrance is a small gate decorated with Fu lions and statues of the protective guardian spirits. The size of the gate with its brown tiled roof conceals the size of the complex found on the other side. Emily moves through the wooden doors to the front hall, where the first gold-covered Buddha statue blesses visitors as they enter. Bright fruit, flowers and incense sit on the altar in front of him, and people stop to pray and bow before moving past into the large courtyard beyond.

The temple seen today was mostly built during the 11th and 12th century C.E. In the early 1000's, Abbot Shourong set out to expand the monastery and community of one hundred monks. They built the central library hall to hold their collection of 5,048 volumes of sutras. In the 1100's the main halls were expanded, a treasury hall was built, the three gold-plated Buddha statues were placed in the Western hall and the gate was constructed. A benefactor paid for needed repairs to the library hall[1].

Though most of the buildings seen today are only 900 to 1,000 years old this temple, also known as the Temple of Bright Filial Piety or Kwong Hau Temple, is the oldest and largest Buddhist temple and worship site in Guangzhou[2][3][4]. The site was originally used as a palace for then-prince Zhou

Jiande, the last king of Nanyue. It was destroyed to make way for the Faxing monastery, an early name for the Guangxiao temple. The main hall was built on the site where scholar Yu Fan (174-241) taught. In 401 C.E., the first notable temple structure still standing was built by an Indian monk named Dharmayasas[5][6].

The flow of Buddhism into southern China came from India through Vietnam, Thailand and Cambodia. The arrival of another Indian monk, Paramātha, in 546 heralded the most significant growth in Buddhism in China. He arrived in Guangzhou and took up residence in Guangxiao. He brought 240 bundles of sutras and a style of teaching that would lead to the school of Buddhism known as "the school of specific characters of knowable things" which focuses on analyzing knowable things instead of abstract absolutes. He brought yogic practices to the region and produced a series of fabricated "translations" of teachings of the Buddha that were popular with mid-sixth century Chinese[7].

Now the main temple complex is a large rectangular courtyard with buildings set at the edges. The center is open and filled with raised tree beds and shrubbery. A drum tower and bell tower face each other across the central axis. On less busy days, it's possible for visitors to hear the nuns, monks and other faithful chanting the sutras in the drum tower. Today the monks, dressed in maroon robes, are helping guests, selling incense clusters, clearing the altars when they get too full and completing the other tasks needed to maintain an open temple and working monastery.

Emily moves to the side of the courtyard and takes time to enjoy the special trees planted here. "The trees are more than three hundred years old," she says. "They will put a plaque on there to tell how old is this tree and what's the tree's name and what's the relationship with this tree and the buddhist." Birds sing here and the air is cooler than outside the temple walls due to the heavy shade. She moves back to the center pathway and passes the good luck incense burner. It's a tall, bronze structure of several levels into which people throw coins. They try to get their coin to stay in the highest level. The burner, like many of the statues and other free-standing pieces, has a protective railing around it so people don't crowd too closely and damage it during the holiday season.

People gather at the three entrances to the main hall where the two-story golden Buddhas sit. Usually there are kneeling cushions placed inside the door and the faithful step over the six inch (15cm) doorjamb to reach them[8]. Fear that crowds will damage the hall changes this practice during the holiday. The cushions are placed on the outside and visitors must move around others using them. The leather cushions are dented and grooved with wear. The main hall also holds the monk's benches and regular worship items.

Emily points to a flower-covered exterior altar, "The flowers came from the people who came here to pray to the gods and ask for the god to bring them happiness and life...I think it's very different from the Western people." She watches as a monk helps a woman with her bag of offerings. Fruit, especially oranges which carry special meaning during the Chinese New Year, are piled on the altars. "All kinds of fruit you can bring here," says Emily before joking that, "maybe durian is forbidden. It's too strong. Maybe the Buddha doesn't like this."

Behind the main hall is a series of smaller halls and galleries used by the monks for daily life and one of the famous iron pagodas. Near the end of the Tang dynasty (618-907), a southern uprising led by Huang Chao saw Guangzhou fall in 878. The city was looted, and an Arab traveler, Abu Zaid Hassan, recorded a massacre of 120,000 inhabitants[9]. A

Guangzhou – Heart of the South

semblance of peace was restored in 907 when the Liu family took control and set up the Nan Han kingdom, or Southern Han, which would last until 960. During this period, the Liu family dedicated itself to building and maintaining Buddhist monasteries. A royal princess would join the Baozhuangyan Monastery – one of the first names of Liurong Monastery. During this period, the king and a royal eunuch each had an iron pagoda built. They were gold-plated and placed in the monastery as a dedication to the Buddha. A show of the wealth and power of the short-lived kingdom[10].

One iron pagoda is standing near the wall at the back of the main temple. "Now you just can see three levels of it. It used to have seven levels, but they did not keep it very well, so now you can just see it like this," says Emily. Designed like a square-tiered wedding cake, it's covered in small carvings of Buddhas. All of the gold is gone[11][12][13]. Most visitors pass it without paying much notice or realizing its value. The second pagoda sits on the other side of the temple, and is generally ignored by visitors because of its placement between side buildings.

Visitors move east down a sloped walk towards a long, two-story building with a series of rooms along the front. Each room is filled with wooden cards hanging on the walls, each with a name of a dead family member written on it. "Maybe the family thinks that here is the temple and a lot of monks will pray for the Buddhists and when they [the dead] are here they will think it is peaceful and they will go to the heaven quickly," says Emily. She stops to look at the fish ponds across from the hall and the woman selling goldfish in bags. The tradition is to release the fish into the pond, which shows mercy and can bring good luck. Emily explains that the fish are scooped up each night and resold the next morning.

Leaving the Quangxiao temple through a side gate,

Emily heads one block east towards Liurong Temple and the famous Flowery Pagoda. The two are sister temples. Liurong is decorated with strings of red lanterns for the holiday. Yellow tassels and small paper signs dangle from each lantern. "Who wants their family to have happiness and keep healthy in the coming year, they buy these lanterns and write down their wishes in there, put it around the pagoda," explains Emily. She says that the price isn't cheap, but all the lanterns have already been bought. The closer to the pagoda or the main temple hall the lantern hangs, the higher the price. The luck it brings will be better she says.

Liurong Temple, or The Temple of the Six Banyan Trees, was built on the foundations of an earlier temple. The Temple of Solemnity and Sarira Stupa, was built in 537 C.E. by the order of Emperor Liang Wu. That temple was destroyed by fire in the early Song dynasty (960-1279) and rebuilt in 989. It is the rebuilt temple, initially named the Temple of Tranquility, which visitors see today[13][14]. The pagoda was built in 1097 with a thousand Buddha images inside, earning it the name "Thousand Buddha Pagoda"[15][16]. The fame of this pagoda spread after the famous writer Su Dongpo visited in 1100. He was struck by the beauty of the six Banyan trees planted in the courtyard beside the pagoda, and wrote the inscription "Liu Rong" or "six banyan trees" on a tablet which has inspired the temple's present name[17]. The tablet can still be found in the temple grounds.

The entrance of the temple leads directly towards the pagoda, with its traditional Chinese-style mini-roofed tiers. The pagoda is an octagon standing 187 ft. (57m)[18]. It appears to have nine stories, but inside there are seventeen[19][20]. The name Flowery Pagoda was adopted as people noticed how bright and beautifully painted the exterior was[21]. Emily notices the colors are simple red, green and white today. "It needs to be rebuilt, but before that they need to report to the government and let some experts do some research and then have a plan on how to rebuild it," Emily says after asking a monk why it's not more brightly painted.

Visitors who walk around the pagoda find the Grand Hall squatting in the shadows. The hall hides behind the pagoda until visitors are almost at the front door. It is 984 sq.ft. (300sq.m) and stands 45 ft. (14m), but appears short in the shadow of the pagoda[22]. The three bronze statues inside were cast in 1633. They are the largest existing ancient bronze statues in Guangdong province[23][24]. Visitors often miss this hall, opting instead to walk the more visible path leading to the other half of the temple complex.

"Compared with Guangxiao Temple...I think the spirit is the same," says Emily as she moves past the ancient trees and halls. She adds that Liurong is less important and smaller than Guangxiao. The courtyard-half of the temple is the Banyan Garden. Here the two remaining banyan trees planted at the time of the temple's founding live. Younger trees, only one or two hundred years old, provide shade throughout the courtyard. Smaller halls box the courtyard. They are dedicated to notable priests or monks who served the temple in past centuries[25].

After visiting this smaller temple most visitors head home, but these temples are not the end of Yuexiu district's offerings. Leaving Liurong and walking two blocks south and one block east, Emily finds the Huaisheng Mosque, the Memorial of the Holy Prophet. It's down a small side street across from a halal restaurant. The top of the broad white minaret pops above the wall of the mosque and the green tiles of the small front gate. Emily watches as a bus full of women wearing head scarves hop off and head inside. It's a, "Muslim temple, but unfortunately this is not for the public. So we just can go around outside, inside is forbidden," says Emily as she cranes her head to get a view inside the courtyard. Only the faithful are allowed inside[26].

The area of the city visitors are now standing in was the heart of the foreign quarter in the city since at least the Song dynasty (960-1279). Seafaring Arab traders landed in Guangzhou well before 700 C.E. They followed the sea route across the Indian Ocean and up the China Sea. The prefect of Guangzhou, Lu Jun, wrote towards the end of that century, "The barbarians lived among and intermingled with our people, intermarried, and occupied land and houses." In the 700's this section of Yuexiu was outside the city walls to prevent traders having direct access to the city. During the Song dynasty, the city walls were expanded, in part because the Arab community paid for the construction to ensure their own protection[27].

The mosque is thought to be the oldest in China and one of the oldest in the world[28]. Built during the Tang dynasty (618-907) when Sa'ad ibn Abi Waqqas, a companion of the Prophet Mohammed P.B.U.H., came to Guangzhou in the 650's[29][30]. The minaret of this mosque was also used as a lighthouse for Arab trading vessels coming up the river to port. It gives this temple its other name – Guangta Mosque or Light Tower Mosque. The tower stands 119 ft. (36.3m) and was once sitting on the bank of the Zhujiang River[31]. The river is now several blocks further south due to natural events and land reclamation projects.

Emily walks back to the main road and continues one block south to the converted Taoist temple Wuxianguan, the Temple of the Five Immortals. "I think this temple can explain why Guangzhou also has another name 'City of Five Rams'", she says. The entrance is a long wall with a three-tiered gabled front door. It's protected by stone statues of the mythical kylin.

These ancient stone beasts with their deer antlers, cloven hooves and fish-scale covered bodies have stood guard for centuries as the city prospered[32].

Upon entering, visitors can choose to wander through the flower and city story exhibits set to the left and right of the hallway or move forward into the main temple area. Emily chooses to move towards the main courtyard and save the other exhibits for last.

The courtyard leads to stairs and the Rear Hall. This hall was facing the river, the museum entrance is placed at the back of the old main temple. It is one of the few palace structures built in the Ming dynasty (1368-1644) still in existence in Guangzhou. The Rear Hall is the only part of the original temple still standing, the rest was destroyed in a fire in the late 1800's[33].

Along the wall of this rectangular room is a modern relief carving of the Five Immortals. According to the museum, "Legend has it that in about the ninth century BC, five immortals dressed in clothes of five colors, each riding a goat and grasping rice ears, descended upon the city. They presented the rice ears to the local people with their good wishes for everlasting prosperity and good harvesting. The immortals then rose into the sky." The goats supposedly turned into stones, and were placed in the temple built where the immortals ascended[34].

Visitors step through the back doors on either side of this statue and are faced with the steps leading to the First Tower of Lingnan. "A bell tower, which was built in the Ming dynasty, the only one maintained nowadays," Emily says. The red windowless, square tower was used as the water gate for the city wall. It was built in 1374, when the walls of the city were expanded[35][36]. "It's very important for Guangzhou. If the enemy goes in through this gate it means Guangzhou belongs to them," she explains.

The tower was built with a domed interior roof to create a resonance chamber which amplifies sound. Inside the tower is the largest bell in Guangdong. Cast in 1378, it has a sinister reputation for causing tragedy throughout the city[37][38]. Diseases that killed children, fires and the fall of the city to the British during the Opium Wars were all blamed on the ringing of the bell[39]. The resonance of the chamber and size of the bell ensured that it could be heard throughout the city when it did ring. Today, it does not have a clapper, ensuring it cannot ring – just in case.

Behind this tower is a small courtyard filled with statues of goats and stone tablets, a pleasant dead-end. Visitors have to back track through the tower to reach the larger courtyard on the side. Here, the "footprint of the immortal" is set off from the rest of the park-like area with a decorative iron fence. "He must be a giant. How can the footprint be so big, like this? I think this is just a legend," Emily says. The footprint, pressed into solid rock, has filled with water. Turtles now call it home. Emily jokes that people put the turtles there just to give them a swimming pool.

Walking through the courtyard Emily passes benches where other visitors are sitting down and enjoying the afternoon. Bronze statues of everyday life are nestled in the shrubs. The olive seller, part of the traditional stories told around the city, rides his bronze rooster in one corner. He is talking to two small children who have come begging for his sweets. In the summer, some people dress up as him and give away candies in the parks.

The back half of the park has a covered walkway that displays replicas of photographs and paintings of Guangzhou life in the Qing dynasty (1644-1911). A little pond separates the walkway from a small sand island. A pottery model of the city as it was during the Tang dynasty (618-907) sits on the island[40]. The walls of the city are clear and visitors can get an idea of how small Guangzhou was until very recently.

The walkway ends with the Museum Temporary Exhibition Hall, a two-story building with green tiles and red woodwork made in the style of an expensive home. The small exhibit space hosts a changing display of local artifacts from Yuexiu district[41]. "In this museum we can see the daily life of the people," says Emily. "The ancient people were wiser than nowadays," she says, looking at the construction style of the past. "They didn't rely on nails."

She moves back through the courtyard and towards the entrance. The last two exhibits, Flower Story and City Story, are waiting for her on either side of the main hallway. Both exhibits use photographs and illustrations to explain their topic. "Every citizen likes flowers, that's why we have another name, 'The Flower City'. And because the climate in Guangzhou is suitable for the plants to grow up," she says moving through the exhibit. The other hall has a large map which lights up to show the growth of the city over the different dynastic periods. She wanders through the rooms and then heads for the door. "I think for me this temple is more important than the Guangxiao temple or the Liurong temple," she says thinking about the benefits provided by the immortals.

Visitors who don't want to end their day just yet could continue south to Haizhu Square. Three blocks south of the Temple of the Five Immortals is the Catholic Cathedral of the Sacred Heart of Jesus, the gothic cathedral created in France, shipped and assembled in the late 1800's[42]. Follow the river west two-thirds of a mile to Shamian Island, where foreigners lived after the first Opium War – including Mrs. Gray.

Mrs. John Henry Gray to her mother excerpted from her book *Fourteen Months in Canton* published in 1880 and now in the public domain.

Letter XXI -

Canton, August 30, 1877
My dear Mother,

I always have so much to describe when I sit down to write you an account of what I have seen in the city, that I must necessarily omit much. As we are going along the streets I feel engrossed in all I see around me, and I am often calling upon Henry for an explanation. This is rather difficult, as, if we are in chairs, it takes some time for me to make the coolies ahead stop, and we often have passed the particular spot or shop before I make Henry hear.

If we are walking we are rarely side by side. The streets are so very much crowded and there is seldom room for us to be together; if we walk abreast for a few minutes, we are sure to be interrupted by an itinerant pork-seller, fishmonger, or some man carrying a burden, who cries out, "Clear the way." Very often it is a chair for which you have to stand on one side, the coolies sometimes calling out "Make way, a great physician is in our chair, who is on his road to see a dying patient." This cry Henry knows to be not strictly true at all times, as the coolies have resorted to it when carrying him in haste to some particular spot.

The streets are also a snare to me: I have to look where I am going, for the granite slabs by which they are paved are most uneven; in fact there is no pretence at using any particular sized blocks of stone; so if one is not careful one may catch one's heel in a piece of stone standing high above its neighbour.

The bridges are numerous in the city, and are generally approached by steep stone steps. They please me very much by their quaintness, and the Chinese in their large pointed crowned hats, their tails, and flowing robes, look most picturesque as they cross them. They are most varied in design, some being very much raised in the centre, others flat.

In one of our walks, a few days ago, we saw a great many sights which came in our way, and we spent the day in the city and its suburbs. The first halt was made at a Chinese dispensary, where three or four native physicians give advice gratis from eight A.M. to two P.M. daily. A ticket is handed to each patient, which is given up by him on receiving advice. Small sums of money and rice are also given here, to aged and poor widows. Four free schools also receive pecuniary assistance from this dispensary, and coffins too are provided for paupers.

On coming out of the dispensary we saw a group of men playing at cards in the street. The players were squatting on the ground with a board in front of them, and men interested in the game were looking on. The cards used by Chinese, and with which they play a great variety of games, are about the same length as European cards, but they are very narrow, being scarcely an inch in width. I have often seen groups of men playing at cards in the streets, and so absorbed were they in their game as to be utterly regardless of the busy crowds around them.

We went into one of the opium divans which is close to the dispensary, and saw men in all stages of stupor from smoking the drug. It was a most revolting sight, and I turned with disgust from the man who was supplying the opium to these poor creatures. Wooden couches are placed round the room, upon which these infatuated men lie and inhale the poisonous drug. Many of them had a most attenuated appearance. When once opium smoking has become a confirmed habit, the victim is utterly wretched if he, by any circumstance, should be unable to indulge in his opium pipe at the customary hours. When walking along the streets the other day, we met a man who had evidently been deprived of his opium pipe beyond the usual time; his distress was most evident, and as he went along towards the opium divan his moaning was most painful to hear.

We walked on afterwards to see the beautiful French cathedral, which was begun in 1863 and is not yet completed. It is built of granite, and is a noble specimen of Perpendicular Gothic. One is surprised to find this fine cathedral within the walls of the heathen city. There are schools and an orphanage in connection with it. The present bishop has resided in Canton upwards of thirty years, and is much beloved by his co-religionists. The French cathedral, schools, etc., occupy the site on which the palace of the Viceroy Yeh formerly stood.

In marked contrast to the cathedral was the building which we next visited, a whitewashed dissenting chapel with bare walls, most uninviting to the passers-by. [Dissenters were British Protestants who separated from the Church of England stating in 1662 and include the Presbyterians, Baptists and Quakers[42].] It must be difficult for the Chinese convert, accustomed as he has been to a high ritual, to much decoration in the temple, and to giving of his substance for the worship of his gods, to understand the motive which influences these Christians to worship God in a meagre house of prayer which costs them as little as possible, and is as plain as hands can make it.

On leaving this chapel we entered the old city, and passed through the street called by Europeans the Bird-cage Walk, in which, as the name suggests, are several shops where birds of various kinds and ornamental bird-cages are sold. I have bought here lately some canaries, Java sparrows, two small birds called nuns, with brown bodies and black heads, two kingfishers, and a blue jay. These feathery creatures, excepting the last two, which are in cages by themselves, are now in my large aviary.

We now entered a street called the Street of Four Monumental Arches, in which we saw five rather than four of these arches, all of them raised to the memory of men celebrated in their day either for learning, virtue, valour, filial piety, or longevity. Monumental arches in China take the place of public statues in European cities, and are generally made of granite, but sometimes of red sandstone or brick. They are built in the form of a triple arch, having in the centre a large gate, and a smaller one on each side. An inscription is placed on a slab in the centre of the large arch, informing passers-by to whose honour the arch is erected. On a small slab, in a prominent position on the arch, are two characters which set forth that it is built by imperial decree.

Having examined these monumental arches, which are now hemmed in at the sides by shops, we passed on and entered the Temple of the Five Genii. (These genii are supposed to represent the five elements, viz., fire, earth, water, metal, and wood.) [Temple of the Five Immortals] These worthies are supposed to have entered the city of Canton riding on rams, and dressed in different coloured robes. On passing through one of the markets they are reported to have said, "May famine never visit the markets of this city," and then they winged their flight through the air.

Five stones formed their resemblance to the rams, and eventually they were removed to this temple. They are arranged at the feet of five well-executed idols, representing the five genii. These idols sit in a row in a large shrine, and are coloured so as to resemble life. Votaries worship here, especially in the fourth month of the Chinese year, when they come to return thanks to these gods for restored health. These votaries then wear a red dress similar to a Chinese prisoner's dress; round their necks are chains, fetters are on their ankles, and handcuffs of iron round their wrists. These strange observances are supposed to indicate humility on the part of the worshippers.

In front of this shrine stands the Great Bell Tower. The Chinese and Tartars [Manchu] are most superstitious in regard to the bell which hangs in this tower, and believe that it has not been struck, since it was cast in 1368, without bringing disaster to the city. An epidemic which caused the death of a thousand children was attributed to this bell having been inadvertently struck. In 1845 the tower having fallen into ruin had to be rebuilt, and the workmen were enjoined not to let the bell be struck as they lowered it to the ground. But with all their caution it sounded out its doleful voice, and the consequence of this was a great mortality amongst the Tartars, and also a fire in a theater, by which three thousand men died. Again in 1865 it was struck by a falling shot from H.M.S. Encounter, and the Chinese attributed the subsequent capture of the city by the allies to this sound of ill-omen.

In one of the courtyards of this temple I saw an impression, on a basaltic rock partly covered with water, resembling the print of a human foot, which is supposed by the Chinese to be the impression of Buddha's foot. You will be amused to hear that there is a small shrine here in honour of a monkey god. He is said to have been formed from a rock, and to have been hatched during the day by the heat of the sun, and during the night by the warmth of the moon. He became in time the king of all monkeys, and, learning the art of speaking he was associated with man, and eventually taken into the service of Buddha.

We went from this temple into the yamun in which the great Viceroy Yeh was captured in 1858 by British sailors. Close to this yamun is the Confucian Temple, approached by a triple gateway built of red stone. In the courtyard I saw an artificial pond, in the form of a crescent, which is spanned by a bridge of three arches. I learnt from Henry that water is always placed in the precincts of a Confucian temple. It denotes purity, and therefore is supposed to be an emblem of the virtue of the sage and of the purity of the doctrines he taught.

In the shrine which stands at the end of the quadrangle an idol of Confucius has been placed contrary to the express teaching of the sage, who was much opposed to graven images. It is more usual to find a red tablet only in a Confucian temple, with the name of Confucius recorded on it in letters of gold.

A long Cloister runs down the length of the quadrangle, and contains small shrines, in honour of the seventy-two disciples of Confucius who shone with pre-eminence out of the number of his three thousand followers. In the inner quadrangle of the temple a shrine is dedicated to the parents and grandparents of Confucius. The Chinese not only honour a great man himself, but they extend their worship to his progenitors, as they consider it is owing to their care and skill that the illustrious man is indebted for his greatness.

We went into a small shrine dedicated to the memory of virtuous women, which is opposite to the Confucian temple. Here we saw many wooden tablets arranged on shelves, which bore the names of women who had spent their lives in single blessedness. A granite arch is raised in this shrine. Other tablets in this shrine record the names of those whose affianced husbands died before the marriage day had arrived, and who passed the rest of their lives in a state of virginity. Other tablets are in honour of windows who refused to marry a second time, or who on the death of their husbands committed suicide, not choosing to survive them. The latter form of suicide is still regarded as meritorious by the Chinese.

We next visited the Mohammedan mosque which greatly resembles Chinese temples in its architecture. It was built by an Arabian in 620, who is said, in Chinese annals, to have been a younger brother of the mother of the prophet Mahomet. As the walls of the mosque are painted red it must have been erected by the sanction of the Chinese emperor then reigning. It is a plain building, bearing above the sanctum sanctorum the first line of the Koran in large Arabic character, "There is but one God, and Mahomet is his prophet." The pulpit is of wood, and a staff is placed near it upon which the preacher leans as he delivers his sermons.

The emperor's tablet stands on an altar in the mosque, and Mohammedans are compelled by Chinese law to burn incense before this tablet, and to worship it. (It is computed that not less than 30,000,000 of China have embraced the Mohammedan faith.) The law commands that this worship to the tablet of the emperor shall be paid in every Buddhist, Taoist and Mohammedan temple in the country. I saw the minaret in the courtyard which was formerly used by the muezzins, who ascended it and proclaimed from its summit the hour of prayer. It has now fallen into decay.

The limit of our excursion this day was the five-storied pagoda, which is built on the heights above Canton. On our way there we turned aside into the street called Chi-Hong-Kai, and entered a small temple to see the prophetic stone which, is supposed to reflect, when gazed upon by those who consult it, what the future has in store for them. Women chiefly visit this temple, and all classes are to be seen here, many of whom consult the stone to know if there is any probability of their earnest longing to become mothers of male children being gratified.

We afterwards passed the Flowery Pagoda. I must describe this most beautiful pagoda to you, as it is one I so much admire and have often seen. It is nine storeys in height; it was built a.d. 505, and was intended as a shrine to hold some relic of Buddha. The original idea in building pagodas was to represent the many mansions into which the Buddhistical paradise is divided. The most virtuous when they die are supposed, as Buddhas, to inhabit the highest place for millions or billions of years – those who are less renowned for their good deeds are supposed to occupy the lower storeys.

Now, however, pagodas are erected by the Chinese for the purpose of exerting a good geomantic influence over the country. Thus, the fields in the neighbourhood of a pagoda are supposed to produce good and abundant crops of grain; the rivers which flow past it to abound with fish; young men who live in its neighbourhood to be successful at the literary examinations; and peace to prevail throughout the surrounding districts.

We went on to the foot of a hill, getting out of our chairs to walk up the long flight of steps leading to the temple dedicated to Koon-Yam. The idol of this goddess is clothed, and in this respect differs from most of the idols in the city [the statue was wearing cloth clothing over her carved clothing]. Her dress is handsomely embroidered. One curious custom is observed in this temple, tradesmen, principally of the humbler kind, as hawkers, barbers, etc., come to it on the 26th day of the first month of the Chinese year, to borrow money from the goddess, as they consider it fortunate to trade with her capital. If the monks of this temple advance five hundred cash to one of these votaries, he must deposit security for six hundred cash, and on the same day in the following year must repay the sum borrowed with a few cash in addition. Men beginning business after the new year consider that money borrowed from this goddess brings luck to them.

We then walked on to the Ng-Tsang-Lau, or Pagoda of Five Storeys [Zhenhai Tower], which stands on the north wall of the city. It is more properly speaking a square tower, and is quite different in shape to the other pagodas in and about the city. It is built of red sandstone or brick, and is a wide building, having five very spacious chambers. I mounted the different storeys, and enjoyed a fine view of the city from the summit. It was here from a temporary scaffold, which was erected on the roof of the tower, that the illustrious Yeh watched the proceedings of his army, with the rebel forces.

During the war which took place between China and the allied armies of England and France, companies of French and English troops on taking Canton were quartered in this tower. We were obliged now to get into our chairs and hurry home through the city, darkness having fallen upon us. You cannot picture to yourself what the streets are like at this hour of night.

The shops are closed, and in some cases are barricaded by long beams. In the principal streets only, small oil lamps hang at intervals from a beam placed across the street; and before the chief shops are large oiled paper lanterns, bearing the name of the hong on one side, and the name of a tutelary deity on the other. These lanterns are most picturesque, varying in size, and shape, and in the characters painted on them; some are very large, others are small. They impart to the streets a most oriental appearance, and it is always a source of interest to me to pass through them when they are lighted up. It is a most curious sight, when entering a long street, to look up it, and see the various coloured lanterns hanging in all directions.

Guangzhou – Heart of the South

At intervals one comes upon the city watchmen, who group themselves round paper lanterns placed on tripods, with the old-fashioned large weapons piled near them. The smaller streets are left to darkness, excepting where paper lanterns hang before the doors of shops, or still larger ones hang before private houses, but these are extinguished by half-past nine p.m.

As we go through these silent, dimly-lighted deserted streets, the footsteps of our chair coolies, and the curious sound they make, a kind of humph! humph! humph! (really a grunting noise), awake the silent echoes. A man every now and then passes us, or perhaps a blind singing girl led by an old woman who conducts and takes care of her. The singer is beautifully dressed, and her hair is bedecked with flowers. Her guide beats castanets to let the inmates of the closed houses know that she and her companion are at hand to be engaged if required. Sometimes the master of a shop calls the girl in to sing to his apprentices, as they work up to a late hour, for, although the shutters are closed, the busy Chinese tradesmen are not idle.

Our way home, this night, led us through a street called Ooi-Sin-Kai, the greater part of which is occupied by blacksmiths. They were working late, and owing to the glare of their furnaces the whole street appeared to be in a blaze. I observed in passing these smithies that instead of two smiths only working together at an anvil, as in England, there were three here, two of whom were using large hammers, and the third a small hammer. Sometimes blacksmiths work in the open air under a wide spreading mat umbrella as represented in the illustration annexed. [The illustration Mrs. Gray mentions has been left out of this book. It is included in her original text.]

The Chinese require little sleep, and can work late and

rise early. I noticed the other day, during one of our early rambles in the city, that the pork butchers were astir before three o'clock A.M.

Chapter 5 – Yuexiu Park

The Yuexiu Park

How to get there: Take metro line 2 to Yuexiu Park stop exit A then turn left.

How much: Park is free. Zhenhai Tower is 10 RMB. Guangzhou Art Museum is 10 RMB.

How long: Half - Full Day

Yuexiu park is a green space for elderly Chinese, young people on dates and anyone who wants a breath of fresh air. It's a park of trees and man-made lakes and home to several museums, famous statues and memorials. Vicky is visiting the park for the first time. "The weather is perfect. It's cloudy but very clear and windy," she says. She's Chinese but lives in Toronto, Canada and has returned to Guangzhou to visit her parents and family. She tries to come every year and is looking for a job so she can stay in the city.

The park covers 212.5 acres (860,000 sq.m) spanning seven hills and has several entrances[1]. The west gate is closest to the metro station and provides easy access to the historical section of the park. The walk here is a broad, shaded path with soft Chinese music piping out of hidden rock-shaped speakers. It follows the edge of a small man-made lake – one of three in the park[2][3]. A family floats past in a rented paddleboat. Older women and men sit and chat on benches. Cards snap down as a group plays a traditional Chinese card game similar to gin rummy. Some men gather around a game of xiangqi, Chinese chess, to observe and comment on the two players' moves.

A sign directs visitors to leave the path and move up the hill if they wish to view the famous Statue of Five Rams. Vicky follows the directions and passes an old man practicing tai chi in a side area. Another man is chanting Buddhist sutras near a rock wall. At the top of this hill path is a wide courtyard. Groups of people are playing a kicking game similar to hacky-sack. The toy used has bright feathers attached to round metal disks stacked together for weight which click when it flies between them – a giant shuttlecock. "People play this as a form of exercise and it's kind of like a social skill. They do it and they talk and a lot of old ladies are also doing it," Vicky says. She admits that she isn't as good as her elders who send the birdy over their shoulders and back and forth with relative ease.

The path winds around the nearby hill. There are two entrances to The Statue of Five Rams. This is the longer route, but it has fewer stairs. At the top sits the famous statue in the center of a circular courtyard. A group of Chinese tourists pose in front of the 36-foot high (11m) statue of cement rams. Erected in the mid-1960's, it became an official emblem of Guangzhou and can be seen on everything from metro cards to tourism signage[4]. "The feeling of it is very strong. Like, the power of the goats or the rams looks very strong. Their standing up and they're in action," Vicky says, "I guess Guangzhou also wants to portray that image to the outside world."

The statue is based on the legend of five immortals who came from Heaven riding rams or goats. Each ram carried six strings of corn millet in its mouth. The strands were planted and Guangzhou prospered. The immortals returned to Heaven; the rams turned to stone[5][6]. Variations of the story are told throughout the city, but the point is the same – Guangzhou is blessed.

In 2010 the Asian Games, the second largest multi-sporting event after the Olympics, were held in Guangzhou. The official mascots were cartoon versions of the statue rams[7]. These athletic cartoons are still seen around the city. The popular children's cartoon, *Pleasant Goat and Bad Wolf* produced in Guangzhou, also pays tribute to the immortal's story.

The other path is a long set of stairs from a lower courtyard to the statue. Guests pass a souvenir and snack shop. At the base of the stairs music is playing from a portable stereo. A group of women are line dancing. "This is like a Chinese aerobics class. There's not really an instructor,…but everybody seems to know what they are doing," Vicky says as she watches the women hop, clap and do jumping jacks as dance steps. A sign points the way towards a stone wall.

This section is all that is left of the protective fortifications built in 1380 C.E. The original Zhenhai Tower was built at the same time. The wall was the most northern edge of the city and was meant to stop bandits and invaders from the north[8][9]. Its gray bricks are now covered in lichen and moss. Several of the local tree species which like to stretch their roots sideways down an open slope to more easily collect rainfall perch at the top of the wall and drape their roots down and even bend them ninety degrees to follow the brickwork patterns. In the shade of the wall and trees, some couples are doing the tango while others waltz.

A raised metal walkway juts out over the hill around the wall's end. One of the five park entrances is below. The walkway bends back and sets guests down on the other side of the wall. From there it's a short walk up the sloping hill to another flight of stairs. Signs here point visitors up to the Sun Yat-sen Memorial. The alternate route, from the Sun Yat-sen Memorial Hall at the bottom of the hill, requires visitors to walk up the "100 Steps" – not an accurate name for the long staircase. The path from the wall avoids most of the stairs and approaches the memorial from the back.

Sun Yat-sen, "The Father of Modern China," is an honored son of the south[10][11]. This two-story, gray stone obelisk-styled tower pays homage to his work on behalf of the region and modern China. Born November 12, 1866 in Zhongshan, Guangdong to peasant farmers, his older brother helped him travel to Hawaii where he began his education. Later, he trained as a doctor in Hong Kong, and become increasingly dissatisfied with the Qing government's lack of adaption to new technologies and modernization[12].

China has always been militarily vulnerable from the sea with most of its urban centers on the coast. The Opium Wars, which destabilized the Qing government, were decided by British naval might blockading the Grand Canal and occupying the major ports[13]. The first Sino-Japanese war (1894-1895) produced a similar outcome and spurred Sun Yat-sen to action against the Qing government[14]. The steps the government did take to modernize only managed to collapse the traditional Confucian imperial system[15]. Unfortunately for the government it did inadvertently succeed in creating stronger "militia armies" – private armies[16].

Militias in Guangdong were not new. Chen Liaocai was praised for raising one in 1804 to stop local bandits, other groups would form during the Opium Wars to oppose the British and French occupation[17]. Sun Yat-sen would try to take advantage of the Qing government's weakness in 1895. He started an uprising based in Guangzhou, but his plans failed. He claimed to have led ten revolts in the years between 1895 and 1911, all of which failed to achieve his ultimate aim of building a stable, nationalist government founded on Western principles[18][19].

In 1911, the Qing government moved to remove several rail lines from service. This spurred the central China provinces to break into revolt and overthrow their provincial governments. Yat-sen was elected the provisional president. He worked to finish off the Qing government and put in place his own group's parliamentary-style constitution-based government[20][21].

The Qing government called on its newly empowered militias, led by General Yuan Shikai, to defend it. Sun Yat-sen bribed Yuan with promises of the presidency of a newly formed republic if Yuan switched sides. Yuan accepted and forced the child emperor to abdicate the throne and end the Qing dynasty. Yuan now had control of the government and the largest army in China. Almost immediately he dismissed the elected parliament and ignored the constitution[22][23].

By 1913, Sun Yat-sen was calling for a "Second Revolution" to topple Yuan who had proclaimed himself emperor[24][25]. Only a few southwestern provinces answered his call: Yunnan, Guangxi, Guizhou, and Guangdong rose again in 1915. Led by Yunnan, the newly formed National Protection Army revolted[26]. Sun Yat-sen set up an alternate government based in Guangzhou and called for the organization of a constitutional protection movement which would restore the earlier republican constitution and recall the dismissed national assembly[27][28]. This led to the North-South war which was ended when local generals carved up China into personal fiefdoms – the "Warlords period"[29].

Sun Yat-sen tried again in 1924 with a partnership

brokered by the Soviet Union in 1923 between his Nationalist Party and the Chinese Communist Party. The CCP had been formed in 1921 by Chen Duxiu, Mao Zhedong and others. Together the two groups created a constitution based on the Soviet Communist Party's document and began to push the northern-based warlords out of power. Sun Yat-sen died in 1925, replaced by Chiang Kai-shek[30][31][32].

Yat-sen did not see the success of the military campaign a year later, or the creation of the modern Chinese system or the shift of power from the south to the north[33]. It was his drive to help modernize China that made him a symbol, and his devotion to the south that made him a hero in Guangzhou[34].

His memorial stands at the top of the tallest hill in the park. Visitors entering the echoing stone interior are met by a sign asking them to please be quiet as they make their way to the second floor. Vicky stands on the promenade of the second floor and faces the front of the memorial. It's covered in dedication plaques and carved inscriptions. "On this big wall there is a lot of Chinese characters, but I can't read it because it's all in ancient language," she says. She points to one section, "Here it says something about forty seasons and the second line says something about forty years." She asks the guard to take her picture, then heads back down to the first floor.

Visitors who follow the path down the "100 steps" will find themselves at the back of the Sun Yat-sen Memorial Hall, an octagon-shaped building where concerts and performances are held. The upper floor is a museum dedicated to the life of Yat-sen, but is mostly in Chinese. Guests who wish to stay in the park should follow the side path back around the obelisk.

From here guests can continue up the hill to Zhenhai Tower. The track and field stadium is at the bottom of the hill.

Visitors can look straight down at the green grass rectangle surrounded by the black, oval track. Rounding the crest of the hill, the peak of the tower comes into view. The bulk of it is hidden by a red brick wall which divides the park from the museum.

The current Zhenhai Tower is the fifth of its kind[35]. The original, built here as part of the wall during the Song dynasty (960-1279), was "the first tower of Lingnan." It faces the Lingnan mountains and was the first gate that northern travelers encountered[36]. Atop the hill it has good views of the valleys in several directions. The view has inspired many poems and articles about the landscape going back to the building's first days. Since the Qing dynasty (1644-1911) it's been called one of the eight most beautiful scenic spots in the city[37].

Zhenhai Tower, or the Five-Story Pagoda, looks nothing like the traditional pagodas found in other parts of the city. It's a long, thin, rectangular building painted red with a green-tiled roof over each floor's balcony. It looks more like a palace than a pagoda. During the occupation of Guangzhou in the first Opium War it housed British troops[38][39]. Vicky stops in the courtyard, "it smells very clean and sweet." Honeysuckle trees are planted throughout the garden. Nearby a few kapok trees with their angled and jointed branches are just beginning to put on their new spring foliage.

In another week the kapok trees will be filled with large, bright red flowers. This is the flower of Guangzhou. The kapok is one of the tallest native trees in the region and is called the "hero tree" because it is always striving towards the light. The red color of the flowers is also considered lucky and the petals are edible. People collect them after they fall, dry them and add them to soups and congee, a kind of rice porridge[40]. The trees here frame the front of the tower.

Renovated in 1928 and re-opened as the Guangzhou Municipal Museum, it is one of the earliest museums in China[41][42]. The Municipal Museum also oversees the management of three other museums: The Memorial of the March 29th Uprising Headquarters Museum, the Sanyuanli Anti-British Museum and the Guangzhou Art Gallery. The Uprising Headquarters museum is in the house where Sun Yat-sen worked to organize the 1911 Revolution. The Sanyuanli is in the building where villagers gathered to organize their fight against British troops during the second Opium War. In this building the first important victories against the foreign invaders were planned. The Art Gallery is in the park and down the hill from Zhenhai Tower, the others are outside the park[43][44].

Inside Zhenhai, "There are lots of big models of the city and maps where development has been made," says Vicky as she moves around the displays on the first floor. The floors above focus on Guangzhou's cultural history, but the first is about the city's growth and maritime power. Each floor is filled with glass cases displaying the museum's nearly 1,000 pieces[45]. The stairs at the back of the hall divide visitors into those going up and those coming down, creating a circular flow of traffic on each floor.

Models of wooden boats, ancient jewelry and pottery fill the displays. A Chinese clepsydra sits in a corner of the fourth floor. Though similar water clocks would be invented by the ancient Greeks, the Chinese clepsydra was developed independently[46]. Four large metal water troughs are stacked one above the other and a spout at the bottom of each of the upper troughs allows water to drip at a regular rate from one into the next. Markings on the side of the lowest trough measure the time[47].

A display of clay people catches Vicky's attention.

"There are small statues, um, people in the past, even now some people still do it, they put these small statues in their homes. They're for good luck. A lot of them, these are obviously made by people by themselves. They all stand for different things," Vicky says. She isn't sure what each figure does, but knows that some people put figures of women in their bedrooms to help with fertility. Other displays include "ear cups" for resting chopsticks during dinner. She laughs over the name card of this display, "in English they are calling them 'chopstickers'. That's really cute."

The fifth floor allows visitors onto the balcony. Heavy wires form a barrier against falling or jumping from the railing. At one end of the balcony sits a man behind a sales counter. He gives Vicky a quick history lesson about the 19th century cannon sitting in the courtyard below. There are two types of cannon: the Dutch-made and the Chinese-made. The Dutch cannon are of higher quality steel, use a rifling technique in the barrel and a breach loading system. This means they safely shot farther and with greater accuracy than their Chinese counterparts. The smaller Chinese cannon were made from low-grade steel, have smooth barrels and are muzzle loaded. He also tells her to return next week when the flowers bloom. The kapoks' tops are at eye-level here.

The view from the balcony is filled with green hills. To the north is Baiyun and the Lingnan mountain range. Sparsely populated, the trees cover the land. Straight ahead, the top of Sun Yat-sen Memorial pops up from the trees on an adjacent hill. The tomb of the Nanyue king can be seen also. The south is filled with buildings of Yuexiu district. The sprawl is moving north.

Leaving Zhenhai Tower, sings point visitors down the hill towards the Art Gallery, a wide, white building with tiled roof and empty front courtyard. It closes for lunch between

11:30a.m. and 1:00p.m. Vicky arrives at just past noon and decides to continue down the path rather than wait for the doors to open.

The gallery is home to the Gems Left by Overseas Trade exhibit and the Earth and Evolution of Life exhibit. The trade exhibit focuses on the major exports of Guangzhou and the region, especially during the Qing dynasty[48]. Large silk samples and a silk loom fill part of the first hall. A description of the pottery kilns, or "dragon kilns," found in Foshan along with some of the works created fills the upstairs gallery.

Pottery in the Qing dynasty was a multi-million dollar industry[49]. Foshan capitalized on the good quality clay in the region and easy shipping by building "dragon kilns." These long, low kilns were built on the side of a hill. New pottery pieces were placed at the top of the kiln on shelves and then the entrance was bricked over. The heat at the bottom of the kiln would rise and dry the pieces. After several weeks, they were moved to a lower area in the kiln. This process was repeated until the pieces were directly above the heat of the constantly fed wood fire. The process took an average of three months. Today, only one "dragon kiln" is still in operation in Foshan.

The other half of the park is home to paved walking trails and picnic areas. This half of the park has little of historical value, but it does have the other two lakes surrounded by shade trees. "It's huge and a lot of people are here to exercise, and to socialize, to play games, to play cards, to gamble. That kind of thing. And it's educational," Vicky says of the park. She's spent a few hours walking around the ponds and up and down the hills. "It's really relaxing."

Guangzhou – Heart of the South

Mrs. John Henry Gray to her mother excerpted from her book *Fourteen Months in Canton* published in 1880 and now in the public domain.

Letter XXXVII -

Canton, March 26th, 1878
My dear Mother,

We had a very pleasant Chinese luncheon-party two or three days ago. Amongst our guests was our friend Mr.'Ng, who has the beautiful house and grounds at Honam. You can imagine the size of his residence, when I tell you that it takes two hours to go over the house, and its numerous gardens and garden houses. He was accompanied by three of his friends, one of whom was an ex-chief justice of the vast province of Szecheun, which in area is larger than England. He filled a most responsible and high position. I could only wonder, as I looked at him, how many miserable prisoners he had condemned to be executed. He is a fine-looking man, and the dress he wore was very handsome. His long, dark rich brown silk coat was lined throughout with fur; he showed us this fur lining when we pressed him to sit near the fire.

It is by thick clothing that the Chinese protect themselves from cold. Fire-places are not allowed in any of the houses, kitchens alone excepted, for fear of the harm that might ensue, in case of accident, to neighbouring dwellings in the narrow and thickly-populated streets. Small charcoal fires, enclosed in bronze or earthenware pans, are used by the Chinese in very cold weather. These portable fires are placed generally in the centre of the sitting-rooms, and the members of the family congregate around them.

The chief justice had very long nails on four of his

fingers; they were from two to three inches in length. I cannot understand how he and others who have these very long nails preserve them from injury, as they do not wear shields over them in society. At night, however, they enclose them in silver or bamboo tubes.

I sat at table with our Chinese guests, Henry having explained to them previously, that it is the European custom for the ladies to dine with the gentlemen of their families. The chief justice sat by my side at the top of the table, and Mr. 'Ng was on my left. We gave an European luncheon, only taking care to have no beef on table, and to have the soup made of chicken. Before our guests touched the soup, they asked the question, "Is there any beef in it?" It is against the teaching of Confucius to eat oxen; he forbids his followers to do so on account of that animal's usefulness in the service of man. Our Chinese guests expressed great satisfaction with pork chops, and also with pancakes and plum pudding which we had provided for them.

Before our friends arrived, a large box containing a present from the chief justice was sent to us. Two sets of silk costumes were in the box, one for our little boy and one for our little girl. [The Gray family had recently increased from two to four with the birth of their twins.] In the former the coat was a bright green, and the trousers a brilliant red. The jacket for our baby girl was violet, and the trousers were green. A little cap of many colours for the boy, with a row of silver-gilt figures to wear round it, and a bright coloured head-dress, to be worn round the forehead (the top of the head being uncovered,) for our little girl, accompanied the other garments. There were also silver-gilt bangles, and a pair of jadestone bangles, both very small in size, for immediate use, a silver chain and an ornament in silver, representing the Ki-lun, or fabulous animal, for the boy's neck, and a Chinese lock on a tiny silver chain for our baby girl. Two card-cases of carved sandal-wood completed the present.

When we thanked the mandarin for his handsome gift, he said in true Chinese style, "it is only a very small present, indeed it is but a trifle." He fortunately is a native of the province of Canton, so Henry and he kept up a conversation together, whilst Mr. 'Ng did his best with me in pigeon English. It was most embarrassing to have the chief justice at my side, and not be able to say a word to him.

I have told you before how much literary degrees are valued in this country. To whatever class a man may belong, if he attain the B.A. degree, or still more the M.A. degree, he is at once raised in social position. A man who takes his Doctor's degree confers an honour on his whole clan, and becomes a man of distinction. Therefore, when these gentlemen on inquiry learned that Henry had taken his Doctor's degree, it not only raised him but also me in their estimation. They at once rose, chin-chinned Henry, and turning to me addressed me as "Taai-Taai," a higher title than "Nai-Nai."

I have not yet told you, I believe, that some few days ago we received a congratulatory present from a military mandarin. It not only consisted of silk clothes, bangles and ornaments for our children, but also comprised a large packet of sugar, another of preserved fruit, a third of a different kind of fruit, and a small chest of tea. All the presents were done up in red paper, and visiting cards of the mandarin accompanied them.

After our Chinese guests had left, we went in our sampan to Paak-Hok-Tuung, and walked thence to Haang-Kau-Oha-Shaan, where there is a small tea plantation. The tea shrub is an evergreen and greatly resembles the box-tree with which we are so familiar in England. It grows to a height of two of three feet. We saw men and women putting them into baskets which they held in their arms. I noticed that they used great care, picking one leaf only at a time from the shrubs.

On the following day I had an opportunity of visiting a tea-factory, where I saw the process of picking out stems and bad leaves from quantities of tea spread on ruttau-trays. This was done by women and girls who employed both hands at a time with great dexterity. In another department of the factory, I saw men sieving and winnowing tea leaves, the machine used for winnowing being precisely similar to the machine employed by English farmers in winnowing grain. In another department through which we passed, men were casting tea leaves into large immoveable fire-pans, rendered hot by charcoal fires. To prevent the leaves from burning, they continually stirred them up with their hands.

The men, who were very scantily clothed, were dripping with perspiration whilst engaged in this work. I was somewhat startled on seeing the means used to make Canton green teas. To produce the colour, Prussian blue and turmeric were mixed with the tea leaves. Gypsum was also added, and when I asked the reason why this was done, I was told that it was to give a pimgent flavour to the mixture. [pimgent is an alternate spelling of pigment and here refers to the adding of green coloration to the tea.] We finally went into the packing room, and I was much amused at seeing men pressing tea into tea chests by means of their naked feet.

We arrived at Canton last year just too late to see the State worship and other ceremonies observed by the mandarins at the opening of the ploughing season. We resolved, therefore, to attend them this year, and hearing a few days ago that they were to take place yesterday, we made all the necessary preparations for a visit to the Sin-Nuung-Taau, a temple dedicated to the god of agriculture, where they were to be held.

We arose at two a.m., and went in a sampan to a

landing-place within half a mile of the temple. When we left the boat it was very dark, and we had to walk over some broken ground, which was attended with difficulty, our only light being a large paper lantern, on which our surname and address were painted in big red characters. We afterwards met several Chinese gentlemen who were on the same errand as ourselves. Their attendants were bearing lanterns before them, as in China no one is considered respectable who goes out after dark without a lantern.

On approaching the temple, we passed, at intervals, groups of soldiers squatting round large lanterns placed on tripods. They were awaiting the arrival of the great mandarins. Their piled arms, consisting of matchlocks, spears, and battle-axes, with gay banners arranged behind them, looked most picturesque as seen by the dim light of the lanterns.

Looking into the temple, we saw in the centre of the quadrangle a high stone dais or altar, upon which sacrifices of sheep and swine, and offerings of fruits were placed. At length, all the officials arrived, and upon entering the temple at once engaged in worship.

As the temple, which is very small, was overcrowded and stiflingly hot, we quickly withdrew and seated ourselves on a bench at the gates of the Wing-Shing-Tsze, or "City of the Dead," which was close by. It was a strange, weird-looking scene upon which we gazed; daylight was gradually approaching, and we could just distinguish the sacred storks (or night herons as they may be called) flying to and from their nests in the thickly-wooded grove of the City of the Dead behind us. It was now five o'clock, and we saw many labourers going to their daily work, and several market-gardeners passed us, carrying the produce of their gardens towards the city.

They were evidently amused at our appearance, as they

all turned round and stared at us. Several lepers, having the loathsome appearance, also passed the place where we were sitting. They came from some mat huts erected for them on the top of a neighbouring hill by humane persons, there being no room for them in the asylum for lepers. These unfortunate creatures had not come to see the State ceremony which was then being held, but to await the arrival of funeral processions passing from the city to the neighbouring cemeteries, with the view of extorting money from the mourners. This custom is practiced daily by lepers.

Immediately in front of us there was a small field, belonging to the temple of the god of agriculture, irrigated and made ready for ploughing. It was intersected by nine long narrow wooden platforms, each of which was raised about a foot from the ground and covered by a mat roof. The mandarins, when ploughing, walked along these temporary platforms, and so avoided the mud and slush with which the paddy field was covered. Nine peasants dressed in yellow now brought red ploughs into the field, to each of which a buffalo was yoked. No sooner were these preparations completed than a stir amongst the soldiers on duty at the gates of the temple showed that the officials had finished their worship.

We, therefore, took our position close to the platform on which the Viceroy was to walk while ploughing his furrows. We now observed that all the officials, attended by a number of singing boys wearing yellow robes, were coming towards the field. The Viceroy and governor were conducted to the two centre platforms; the Tartar General, the Provincial Treasurer, the Chief Justice, the Literary Chancellor, and three other officials, occupying the side platforms. These nine high mandarins were dressed alike in robes which are only worn on this and similar occasions. The robes were long, made in dark blue silk, with patterns of dragons on them worked in gold thread. They were tucked up in front by belts worn round the waist. The costumes were completed by court hats trimmed with red floss fringe.

Each official carried a small wand in his hand, which was wound round by silk threads of five colours. These wands were supposed to represent whips. The singing boys now arranged themselves on the banks of the paddy field, and at the command of the master of ceremonies burst forth into hymns of praise. The officials, too, at this moment, placed their hands on the ploughs and began to plough their nine furrows. Each of these State ploughmen was followed by two mandarins, who scattered rice seed from boxes, which they held in their hands. These amateur ploughmen and sowers of seed walked up and down their respective phit-forras nine times, and the ceremony was then brought to a close.

You would have been greatly amused had you witnessed this State ceremony. The officials were brimful of pomposity, walking in the peculiar mandarin gait, with countenances unmoved, all expression banished from them. This ceremony is observed on the same day, throughout the length and breadth of China. The Emperor himself takes part in it, ploughing his nine furrows with a yellow plough. However much we may laugh at some of the details of this singular ceremony, we must acknowledge that a religious feeling has prompted the nation at large to ask a blessing upon the plough and all arable lands of the country. It is of great antiquity, having been observed by the Chinese for several centuries.

On our way to rejoin our boat we met a strange procession of thirty or forty men dressed in long white sackcloth garments, with white bandages, like nightcaps round their heads. They were walking in Indian file [single file] along a narrow bank. We conjectured that they were going to the "City of the Dead" to remove remains of a departed relative to a newly-made tomb in one of the neighbouring cemeteries. Still, these mourners must have been near of kin to the deceased, as sackcloth garments are only worn by those immediately related to the departed one. Friends attending a funeral wear a strip of white cloth only round their foreheads.

Chapter 6 – Baiyun Mountain Reserve

The Baiyun Mountain Reserve

How to get there: Take Bus 24, 240, 285, or Tourism Bus Line 3 and get off at Yuntai Garden Bus Station. Then walk to the right up the mountain or take the tourist cable car.
Or
Take bus 32, 46, 60, 127, 175, 179, 199, 240, 241, 298, 540, 543, 615, 841, or 891 and get off at White Cloud Telpher (Baiyun Suodao) Station. Walk to the gate.
Or
Take metro line 3 to Meihuayuan Station and walk 1,200 meters to the Plum Garden. (Unless you have a Chinese translator to help, this is not an easy entrance to find.)

How much: Park is 5 RMB. Moxing Ridge (Star-Scraping Ridge) is 5 RMB. Guangzhou Forest of Steles is 5 RMB. Xinghai Garden is 3 RMB. Bird Sanctuary 10 RMB.

Cable Car: 25 RMB to go to the top and 20 RMB to go to the bottom.

How long: Full Day

     Baiyun Mountain is a green, wooded space with historic, mostly religious buildings scattered up its sides and along its ridges. It was a holy place in ancient China and is believed to bring good luck to those who climb to the top. Part of the Lingnan mountain range, this park encompasses the "first peak of the south," and the land around it[1]. It is the first mountain peak travelers faced when choosing to go north. The park's other name, White-Cloud Mountain, refers to the English translation of Baiyun. The peak is usually covered in wispy, low-hanging clouds.

"It's a really gorgeous place," says Wilson. He works for the Guangzhou government and is spending a day visiting the mountain. He's brought a backpack and a small umbrella. The weather in the spring and summer is notorious for flash showers. Many residents carry umbrellas to fend off the harsh sun and sudden rains. The mountain air is fresh, but still sticky with the high humidity of a sub-tropical summer.

Wilson has lived in Guangzhou for the past twenty years. He moved here to further his career after finishing university. He studied English after school and enjoys practicing his skills with native speakers. While most visitors start their exploration of the park from the south entrance, Wilson is using the smaller west gate closer to the metro station. It's harder to find than the main gate, nestled behind a neighborhood of twisting streets.

Before getting into the park a sudden downpour forces him to take shelter in a local restaurant. While waiting for the weather to clear, he explains that when someone pours tea locals will often tap two fingers on the table. This is a "thank you" based on the story of an emperor who wanted to go out in secret and meet the people. His servants refused to let him go alone, but they could not kowtow without giving away the secret. They agreed to tap their fingers to secretly show honor to the emperor. Once the rain passes, Wilson strolls to the small west gate. It leads to a set of steep stone steps that twist and disappear among the lush greenery of the mountain.

At the opposite end of the park is the large, broad southern gate. It connects to the main road. Cars can drive all the way to top of the mountain if they enter here. Families and individuals wander in small groups up the sloping path. Signs mark where each interesting building or site is for visitors who want to leave the main road and explore. In contrast, the west gate's stairs are only broad enough for two and are steep, not the gentle slope of the south gate's walk. There are no signs or turn offs. Just as he reaches the top, the rain begins again.

A small cement block building surrounded by bee hives stands near the top of the stairs. The door opens and a man with copper skin, short cropped black hair and forehead wrinkles like pond ripples steps out and waves Wilson into his home. He's a bee keeper and works with the park's honey co-op. His home is littered with daily life. He says his wife and grandson are at the bottom of the hill waiting for the rain to pass. They live together in this cluttered room, taking care of the boy while his daughter works in an office in the city.

As the rain hammers down on the metal roof, he rinses out his one red mug and fills it with loose tea leaves and hot water for Wilson. He is eager to tell the story of his hometown Wenchang – a city flattened by an earthquake. The 7.9 magnitude quake struck at mid-day in May 2008. The poorly built buildings collapsed, burying children at school and office workers. Officially 87,150 people were killed and $137.5 billion USD was needed for repairs. It was the first time in China's history that it requested international aide[2]. The bee keeper thinks about 90% of the people in his city died when the buildings fell. He believes he's alive today because he went to visit a friend in a neighboring city the morning of the earthquake. He also believes that the government covered up the real epicenter of the quake and the damage done and lives lost there because of the location's connections to the Chinese army in the area.

Thirty minutes later the rain is stopping. Summer showers in Guangzhou don't usually last long. The bee keeper leads Wilson to the lookout point at the end of the courtyard near his house. Spreading beneath the mountain towards the river is modern Guangzhou. New, tall buildings hide short, old ones. These vistas are common as the road winds around the mountain.

"Over there is Guangzhou city, Zhujiang New Town. The east tower and west tower. The landmarks of Guangzhou. Especially the Canton Tower," says Wilson as he looks out at the vista. In 1980, visitors would have seen rice paddies, not the central business district (CBD) of Zhujiang New Town, Liede, and Tianhe[3]. The Canton Tower hadn't been proposed yet. The massive university complexes in Haizhu were twenty years away. The city of 1980 had more in common with what captains and seamen of the 1800's saw as they sailed up the river to Guangzhou port.

Peter Parker in his journal dated September 6, 1835 wrote, "I have the last six & thirty hours been passing in view of scenery which in the estimate of the late Lord Napier, 'are worth a voyage from England to see.' On either bank are extensive paddy fields clothed in richest verdure, with here & there a village with its arbor of bamboos. Numerous forts of granite. Beyond the paddy fields the hills & mountains rise in pleasing variety & upon the plains & loftiest eminences the towering pagoda stands – the monument of the ingenuity & enterprise of generations forgotten[4]."

Following the road around the mountain, Wilson arrives at another viewpoint. It looks out over the trees and down to one of the reservoirs. Thin misty clouds float up from the trees like little puffs of steam. "There are two lakes near Baiyun mountain," says Wilson, "the little and big lakes."

They are maintained as recreational areas. He used to visit and relax at a famous restaurant on the bank of the big lake. Their outlets flow into the Zhujiang River. The wide river basin system allowed a relatively safe port to spring up here which made Guangzhou a major player in trade for centuries.

In the Song and Tang dynasties (618-907 and 960-1279), Guangzhou was the most important port in China. Slowly it lost that status, but remained an important export hub and in the mid-1800's it birthed the Chinese Industrial Revolution. Innovation was slow in coming to China, but in the south it took hold with the silk trade.

Chen Qiyuan made his fortune when he brought the silk filature process from Vietnam to Guangzhou in the 1850's. The steam powered machine could unwind several silkworm cocoons at the same time and produced thin, even thread. The speed of production and quality of thread increased silk production in the region. It was the first mechanized production system in China and made Guangzhou the seat for the silk trade for years[5].

Leaving the viewpoint, the path continues to a division. One path leads to a courtyard where visitors riding the cable car are deposited, the other leads to a small ticket counter and a flight of stone stairs. The top of the stairs is hidden by the thick vegetation and mist. These steps go to Moxingling – Moxing Summit. "It's about 382m [1,253 ft.] from the sea level," says Wilson. Moxing Summit is the highest point in Guangzhou[6]. The reason the mountain is named Baiyun "White Cloud" is best appreciated from the summit. "You can see a lot of white clouds. It's amazing." The wispy clouds that circle the mountain are formed by the trees, humidity and the cooler temperatures of the elevation.

"The steps is so many. So much. I almost give up," Wilson says as he climbs the slippery, wet steps. After stopping to catch his breath and look at the view, he arrives at the top. Other visitors are enjoying the 360° views of the city from different points on the peak ridge. A young couple is standing next to one of three posts placed in a triangle. The posts are connected by heavy wires strung between them thickly covered with metal locks. Wilson says, "According to the Chinese, we think that if you make two locks together you will stay together forever. Just make a wish, make a will." The couple snaps their lock over the wire and walk off holding hands.

As visitors move from one half of the ridge to the other, they pass a stone three-arch gate. Set to the side of the path, it honors a former general of the region says Wilson. The path continues and circles the second half of the ridge. Staircases at each of the cardinal points lead up to a courtyard with an open-sided bell tower. The bell has a long striker, like a log, suspended next to it. As its rope is pulled back and released, the striker swings forward and hits the reinforced side of the bell. Visitors are encouraged to wait their turn to ring the bell for luck. "You have one strike to ten strikes. You can have a lot of amazing things. Like make your life better, find you the right one for you, get a lot of money, have a lot of kids, yeah, like that," says Wilson. The number of rings tells the gods what type of assistance is needed[7]. Guests step up in a steady stream for their chance at the bell. The chime is heard across the peak and down into the valleys.

Taking the stairs down to the main park, visitors soon emerge from the green hillside and rejoin the main road. It is green here all year round. Tiny pink and white blossoms can be found wherever a visitor looks. Even during winter there are still usually a few flowers toughing out the chill. Winters in Guangzhou are mostly cool with a few days of cold that can bring frosts, though this is unusual. January is the coldest month with temperatures averaging between 50° and 64.4° F (10°-18° C). July is the hottest and wettest month with average temperatures between 78.8° and 93.2° F (26°-34° C) and 1.18 ft. (360.2mm) of rainfall[8].

The road down the mountainside winds its way over the slopes. It passes the Guangzhou Stele Forest. This was the location of the Baiyun Temple. Built during the Song period (960-1279), it was destroyed during the Second Sino-Japanese War (World War II). The stone stele that now stand here were completed in 1994 and cover 52,493 sq.ft. (16,000 sq.m). There are nearly three hundred steles. Each is engraved with works by famous poets, calligraphers, or information about historic celebrities[9].

Near the stele, farther down the hill is the Nine-Dragon Spring. The spring was a watering spot for the monks who lived on the mountain at Baiyun Temple and Nengren Temple. A statue of nine dragons surrounds the water pool. The dragons' fierce faces and claws are meant to scare away evil and protect the spring.

Europeans generally view dragons as evil, damsel-devouring monsters, like Smaug in J.R.R. Tolkien's *The Hobbit*. They are creatures of earth and fire. In China, dragons are viewed as auspicious and symbolize strength, wisdom, good luck and have power over water and wind. Dragons were thought to rule the rivers and waterways. They also controlled rain and storms. The Dan people and other locals believed that the Zhujiang River was a large dragon who would take the souls of drowned people. Temples around the city were dedicated to the dragons. People prayed for favorable weather and for avoidance of natural disasters[10][11]. The Nine-Dragon Spring of Baiyun Mountain is a part of that tradition.

Visiting each of these areas is a side trip away from the main path. This limits the foot traffic in the smaller areas.

Down the main road a courtyard is located in Dishuiyan Valley, between Nine-Dragon Spring and the TiannenDiyifeng Arch. Snack stands here sell water, souvenirs and ice cream. On one side of the courtyard is the entrance to Mingchungu Natural Birdcage and the other side is the entrance to the most popular viewing area in the park.

Mingchungu Natural Birdcage is the largest natural bird cage in China. The 164,041 sq.ft (50,000 sq.m) park is divided into six areas: the large bird cage area, exhibition of rare birds, birdcage hanging corridor, bird training area, bird specimen showroom and Dripping Rock butterfly house. In the specimen showroom a few stuffed birds sit in glass display cases, but the main exhibit is locked. Visitors follow the sounds of the birds down the path towards the large bird cage. More than five thousand birds, representing one hundred and fifty species, live in the park[12].

The main bird cage is a slice of the hill covered in a large net to prevent the birds from leaving. Stone pathways guide visitors through the area. The walks follow the banks of the man-made pools and water features. Peacocks strut about sounding off. Birds flit in the trees or stroll over the paths and under the shrubs. Illustrated signs placed along the path offer visitors a chance to identify the birds they see in the different areas.

Leaving the bird house, visitors continue on the path to the caged birds, mostly parrots and cockatiels at the other end of the park. This leads past the butterfly house exhibit. Thick chains hang over the doors to prevent the butterflies from leaving the house. "We can't find any butterflies right now. We can just see dead butterflies on the leaves," Wilson says after taking a walk through the butterfly house and not finding a single living specimen.

After the natural birdcage, crowds gather at the

TiannenDiyifeng Arch. Music plays at the top of the stairs behind the arch where the Viewing Scenery in the Evening Platform is located. It's a wide platform with a sitting area on one side and open square on the other. Visitors relax and take in the view of the Guangzhou CBD below. This is regarded as one of the best spots to watch the sunset in Guangzhou[13]. The sky colors the mountains and the clouds, then the city slowly lights up from below. The multi-colored Canton Tower and the IFC building and those around them come to life. Their lights will stay on until around eleven o'clock but Baiyun Park only stays open until 5p.m. For this reason, the light show is best seen in the winter when night comes early.

The CBD is a testament to the continued prosperity of the city, despite setbacks in the past two hundred years. The city suffered after the British love for tea and the Chinese demand for payment in silver lead to the Opium Wars. The first causalities were the citizens addicted to the illegal drug. Tension in the region grew and the first shots of the first war were fired in the Guangdong countryside[14]. The British invaded the city in 1841. They threatened to bomb the city from their ships if a payment of six million yuan was not paid. Among the concessions made to buy peace, the Qing government split Hong Kong from the Guangdong region. This created a British-held trade port and reduced Guangzhou's dominance in the region[15][16][17].

Worse for the city, more opium now flowed up from Hong Kong than ever before. Local leaders, trying to save their people from the drug, started the second war[18][19]. The British invaded the city once more and arrested the Manchu governor-general, the highest ranked political member in the city. The Qing government's total failure to protect the south is why groups like Sun Yat-sen's and the Chinese Communist Party were founded here[20].

From here visitors can go up the hill towards Moxing Summit or down towards Nengren Temple and the south gate. One man on his way up strolls along the road with his stereo playing classical Chinese music without headphones. Another man in his twenties is following an older man down the hill. He is trying to learn how to use a leaf whistle. The older man stops to show him the technique and they continue around a bend in the road making shrill bird whistles together with long blades of grass cupped in their hands. Runners sprint down a series of shallow steps completing the exercise route that spans the park.

A sign points to Nengren Temple through a stone gateway. The temple is a set of buildings pressed back against the side of the mountain. In 960 C.E., the small Yuhong Cave temple was built here. It was replaced in 1851. Those buildings were famous and Sun Yat-sen and his wife, among other notables, visited the site. The temple was destroyed during World War II and forgotten. A tea house took its place in 1949 as local tourists began to return to the mountain[21].

The People's Government of Guangzhou decided to reconstruct the temple in 1993. Though it is based on the temple structures built in 1851 most of the Lingnan decorations and style were not included giving it a more generally "Chinese" feel and less a sense of the region. The seven buildings that make up the temple include the Daxiongbao palace, Ciyun palace, Tianwang palace, Dicang palace, Liuzu palace, a bell tower and a drum tower[22]. "It's also the traditional temple building. It looks great," says Wilson.

The temple is dedicated to Buddhism and the main building houses several statues. The second palace is on the slope above the first and looks out onto the grey, moss covered roof and down towards the valley. The complex covers 32,808 sq.ft. (10,000 sq.m), most of which is taken up by the two main buildings in the central courtyard. The temple is not a major religious site in the city, but is one of the top eight scenic spots on the mountain[23].

Before leaving the temple, Wilson stops to read and explain one of the signs. He says the black stone with gold characters tells the story of a young locally-born monk, Lutzu, who was not well educated. He was tested against another monk to determine who should take over the running of the temple. They were both asked to write a poem about the sacred bodhi tree and the nature of Buddhism. Lutzu wrote, "The bodhi tree is not here. Why are you looking for what does not exist?" His competitor, a well-educated member of the group, wrote, "The bodhi tree is in my heart. I will work to share its wisdom." The second poem was deemed to focus too much on the self. The Buddhist's goal is to give up self and the material world. Lutzu won the contest and went on to become a famous monk and teacher throughout China.

Visitors move towards the exits as the sun begins to set. "I do think Baiyun Mountain park is the name card of Guangzhou city. If you want to know more about Guangzhou city, you should take a trip to Baiyun Mountain, maybe you can get the same feel as the Guangzhou citizens," says Wilson. He hops on a bus as the park closes for the night and heads back to the CBD for dinner.

Mrs. John Henry Gray to her mother excerpted from her book *Fourteen Months in Canton* published in 1880 and now in the public domain.

Letter III -

Canton, April 12th, 1877
My dear Mother,

We paid several calls' on Wednesday, and found most of our friends at home. I was glad to have an opportunity of seeing the interior of the houses in our settlement. I was much struck with their English appearance, carpeted as they are with English carpets, many well-known engravings hanging on the walls. The black wood furniture and the large verandahs alone make one realize that one is in the East, when seated in one of these large drawing-rooms. I think when Europeans return to their native lands, they must feel very much disappointed with the contracted, cramped houses they have to live in.

When our calls were paid, we went into the city, and after a search in some of the curiosity shops for blue china, we entered the Flowery Forest Monastery. The monks were having a meal in the hall, and plentiful the feast appeared to be, with its many dishes containing various portions of food. They rose and welcomed us, and expressed great pleasure in seeing Henry again. We begged them (you can imagine mine was the pantomimic action) to be seated. They offered us seats at another table, and one of the young monks brought us tea in covered cups. Another of them, whose duty it is to receive visitors, sat down with us, and Henry and he chin-chinned each other by touching cups, and then we sipped our tea.

Dried fruit of various kinds, lichees, wampees, dragon's eyes, dried ginger, etc., were placed on the centre of the table in a lacquered box made in many compartments. The monk handed the dried fruit to us on a little two-pronged fork, and opened the dried lichees before he passed them to us. Henry, then, in true Chinese style, took a piece of the dried fruit on the little fork, rose, and put it into our host's mouth. In the meantime the repast was going on at the other table close to us. I should think there must have been some thirty little china bowls, with various kinds of food in them, in the centre of the table.

Meat is forbidden to these Buddhist monks, but it is by no means certain that sundry small pieces of pork or other flesh were not to be found in these little bowls. Each monk had his own basin in one hand, the chopsticks in the other, and he helped himself first to one of the dainties, then to another, from the centre of the table. This is the way all Chinese take their food. When the repast was over, the monks came to our table and stood by us; each then spoke to us, took some morsel from our centre dish, and handed it to us. The dragon's eyes and other kinds of dried fruit were so distasteful to me, that I had to take them slyly from my mouth and hide them in my saucer.

The monks are dirty-looking men, with un-intellectual faces, and the long nails that they wear on some of their fingers look as if they had not seen soap and water for many a long day. They are very courteous, and the ceremony of bowing at each of the little doorways in taking leave of the monk who conducts you to the street, is very wearisome.

On leaving this reception hall we went to see the shrine of The Five Hundred Disciples of Buddha. It is a most extraordinary sight. The figures, which are almost life-size, are made in clay and gilded, and as they have just been restored they are extremely bright. As you enter the shrine you see long rows of these figures, sitting on a raised platform, in lines and cross lines. Each figure represents a disciple according to his idea of sanctity. Some hold their arms upright, which have stiffened in this position; one I saw with both arms so raised; others are in contemplative postures. One carried a crozier in his hand, another had a mitre on his head, while others wore crowns. All are represented as having dark-blue hair, and in some instances the figures have blue beards. No two are alike. In a few cases represented, the disciples being especially holy, a little image of Buddha is formed in the chest, giving a most curious appearance to the idol. The vestments these figures wear are, curiously enough, Catholic in form.

We afterwards passed through the Beggars' Square; here beggars are allowed to assemble, and to sleep, and in case of death are provided with a coffin by the guild of the Fokien merchants [Fokien is a small city in Fujian province on the northeast border with Guangdong[24].] The rules of the beggars' guild are strict, and elders are appointed to enforce them. The beggars are under the protection of special deities.

From the Beggars' Square we returned home. You perhaps can imagine how strange I feel at present in this new life; to be waited upon only by men, not to have a female servant in the establishment, for I have acted on Henry's advice, and have not engaged an amah. He thinks these women given to gossiping, and a great evil in a house. It seems to me as if I were staying at an hotel, as I do not know what will appear at table; nor have I seen my cook, as he does not come into the house. The servants' offices are a low range of buildings joined to the house on the one side.

The singular costume of the servants strikes me much; their queer lingo I cannot understand – naturally they have the same difficulty in respect to my English. Our head boy being asked the other day if he knew what I said, replied, "I no savey, missussi talkee ploper English." Our dining-room is now ready, and I must say our rooms are very comfortable.

I hope the account of my illness, which Henry sent you last week, did not alarm you much. I was very ill at the time, and for two or three days the doctor could not make out what was the matter with me. He looked very serious, and alarmed Henry by saying that he had been called in only just in time. He was surprised at the agony I suffered not lessening with the remedies. At last he pronounced the illness to be caused by paint poisoning, and said that I must, ill as I was, be taken in a boat across the river, and sit for some hours in one of the gardens at Fa-tee, as change of air was really necessary for me.

The marvellous effect that the remedy produced upon me proved that Dr. Brereton was right in his treatment. I was helped to the boat, and could scarcely sit upright, but after I had been in the garden house of our favourite retreat an hour or so I began to feel better, and the miserable feeling of nausea, which had not left me for six days, was sensibly lessened. On my return at night I was much better, and from that time improved rapidly.

My experience of painter's colic is that it is one of the most painful illnesses possible. In my case the fever was so high that in the first night I was seized I became partly delirious. Henry says, in all his experience of visiting amongst the sick at Canton, he has not known any patient so scorched up with fever as I was.

I must now tell you about a day's excursion we made into the country. Do you remember Henry saying, before we left England, that he would take me as soon as possible the forty miles' trip through the valleys encircling the White Cloud Mountains? No European but he knows this route, and he accidentally discovered it some years ago. Two mountain chairs, which are much lighter than those used for the city and level, were brought round to the Chaplaincy at a very early hour yesterday morning. These chairs are made of bamboo rods, and have a covering of dark-green cotton over the head and sides, which can be taken off the light bamboo poles, which support it, at pleasure.

We started immediately after the morning service, a little after nine o'clock. Such a cavalcade we formed, with our fourteen chair coolies and an old coolie whom Henry has employed for years to accompany him in all his excursions. The chair coolies when not engaged in carrying us (we had the double number, Henry eight and I six, so as to have relays) had long bamboo poles resting on their shoulders, from one end of which hung their large circular hats, and from the other end the clothes of those carrying the chairs were suspended. The hats belonging to the chair coolies are either blue, or red and black; they have pointed crowns, and are about the size of a lady's sunshade.

The men, after we had started only wore short dark-blue or brown cotton drawers, reaching to the knee; some had on straw sandals, others walked the whole distance with naked feet. Their brown shoulders glistened in the sun, and my heart bled at the deep-red marks made by the pressure of the chair-poles on them. Imagine any European carrying a burden and walking forty miles in the day, and for half that distance having to share the weight of a chair and its passenger! Our route first took us through the city, then through its suburbs and outlying villages.

The number of Chinese going in the same direction as ourselves was very great, as the worshipping of the tombs had just begun [Qingming Festival or Tombsweeping Day marks the start of spring plowing and planting[26]]. Most of these people were on foot, but some went along in chairs. They carried with them long strings of paper ingots, to burn at the tombs. These ingots, or mock-money, are done up like little sugar-loaves, and are strung on cord. I saw men carrying five or six such long strings of ingots from the end of their bamboos. They also had offerings of cake in red painted boxes, fire-crackers, and bright-colored and white paper, the latter of which they stick in strips on the graves.

I also saw some men carrying roasted pigs cooked whole, for offerings. The Chinese are too thrifty to leave these at the tombs; they merely offer them, then bring them home and feast on them with their relations. All male members of a family must worship their ancestors' tombs yearly, and we met fathers taking their sons of all ages with them to the graves.

But before I say more on this subject, I must tell you what we saw before we reached the place of tombs. When we had passed through the suburbs of the city we came to the asylum, or rather, small village, set apart for lepers. Here one sees the disease of leprosy in all stages; in some cases it is not apparent to the stranger, in others it has assumed a most repulsive form, and is more sad to look upon than anything I had ever witnessed. One young girl had only the stumps of her hands left, and her feet were without toes.

The lepers intermarry, and thus the disease is propagated and increased; it is most sad to see the little children affected by this loathsome disease. [The exact mechanism for transmission of leprosy is still not known. Contact with the infected, respiratory and insect-born transmission are current theories[25].] The Government supports this leper village, but those who are capable of working make ropes, which they sell, and so obtain additional comforts for themselves. These poor lepers have also their temple and their especial god. After walking through this sad place, where all are most anxious to display their deformities to get a kumshaw from the strangers, we got into our chairs.

We next passed by a hill where malefactors who have been decapitated are buried. A stream of people, bearing offerings, was passing on, and others we met were returning empty-handed from the graves. The tombs were soon on all sides of the mountain in stone or asphalte. These belong to the rich; the graves of the poorer class are simply marked by an upright stone or a conical mound of earth. We now heard the report of numberless fire-crackers being let off on all sides to frighten away evil spirits, and this sound continued at intervals the whole day. It gives one the effect of military funerals, as if salutes were being fired over the graves.

The hills were literally covered by worshippers. The tombs do not, as a rule, look imposing, as they are hollowed out of the hills, and with few exceptions are plain. Some have high granite pillars and red flag poles in front of them, denoting the rank of the deceased. A few have rows of animals and attendants carved in stone, which form an avenue, and lead to the tomb of a man of high rank.

We very much enjoyed the country, which became pretty, and in parts really beautiful after we left the city far behind us. On we went past fields prepared for rice, and by small patches of the rice growing thick together, which after a short time will be transplanted, and will be sufficient to cover several acres. We passed by lands prepared for every description of seed. It was most interesting to me to see agricultural labour going on according to Chinese custom. This is of a most primitive kind: they plough with buffaloes; the harrow is most curious, something like a gridiron, and with this they mix the mud and water together to prepare the land for the transplanting of the young rice.

The fields are wonderfully small here, which is partly owing, so Henry says, to the need of facilitating irrigation. The seed is sown by hand. I was struck by noticing a man banking up the earth over some beds containing vegetable seeds. He used a large spade for this purpose, to which a double cord was attached, and a boy standing on the opposite side of the bed assisted the labourer by pulling the spade towards him by the cord. None of these peasants seemed pressed for time; they rise very early and work late, and they look as if they do not know what it is to be in a hurry. We passed by groves and groves of peach-trees, the fruit of which is now set, but will not be ready for the market until June.

At one o'clock we stopped at a farmhouse, where Henry has lunched several times before when he has made this long excursion. How can I describe this strange scene? First, a woman came out, took care of me, and led me into what I thought was a kitchen. In trooped men and boys to stare at me; the little boys only seven or eight years of age amused me, as in most instances they had babies strapped on to their backs. One of these odd-looking little babies was unwound from a boy's back and given me to nurse. The little thing, about six months old, had a silver chain, with charms hanging to it, round his neck, and silver bangles on his arms and legs.

I then joined Henry, who was in the large hall of the house, and I found our coolie placing our luncheon on the table. We were objects of the greatest interest to the whole clan, which was collected in all its force to-day. The family had just returned from worshipping the tombs of their ancestors, and were about to spread their repast in this large hall; but on our arrival they most kindly left it for our use, and themselves dined al fresco.

We must have had sixty persons round us, and when we began to eat they pressed close to us, and were most anxious to see how we used our knives and forks. They would have become troublesome, had not the elders of the clan kept them in order. It was so curious to feel that our ways were looked upon as so barbarous and foreign. Possibly they concluded that when we became more enlightened, we should copy them in the use of chopsticks, etc.

When we had finished our luncheon, we went outside, and found a large gathering sitting on the ground, with the remains of a feast before them. This was the ancestral feast, and is supposed by the people to come direct to them from their ancestors, as the expenses of it are defrayed from the endowment of the ancestral altar. Every member of the clan partakes of this feast, and one of the greatest punishments which can be inflicted on an undutiful son is to prevent him from participating in it.

The country became still more charming after we left the farmhouse, and the mountains and valleys were beautiful with the shades of the sun upon them. We should have missed the finest part of the scenery if Henry had not known the route, as the chair coolies wished to take us direct over a high hill after we left the farmhouse, which would have shortened the journey by some six or seven miles.

They refused to take us where Henry intended to go, round the base of this hill. I got out of my chair and we walked on, the men stoutly declining to give in, and they became threatening in their attitude. When we had walked on a mile (I must own with depressed feelings on my part, as we were at least twenty-six miles from home) the chair coolies, seeing that they could not intimate us, brought up the chairs, and we continued our long journey.

Our way now led us across the large Canton plain, which is highly cultivated, and produces tobacco, cotton, sugar, indigo, rice, and vegetables of various kinds. It was eight o'clock p.m., when we were some five miles from the city, and by this time it had become quite dark. I was in front, and not hearing the voices of Henry's coolies, I became uneasy, and called out to him. No answer came, and I called again.

125

I had been warned by Henry not to show distrust of the Chinese, so, with as cheerful a voice as I could command, I continued to call, but in vain – no answer came. I felt anxious, as just after we started I had been told that I was foolish in going out for an excursion, such as we intended to take, with my gold earrings, locket, and rings all exposed to view. The men too had been so very insubordinate, and one had looked so evil in the discussion of the choice of routes, that I feared something might have happened to Henry. I could neither speak nor understand a word of Chinese, and, therefore, could not tell the coolies to stop, so on we went.

After some ten minutes or more, we came to one of the resting-places erected by some man as a meritorious work, and here I was put down on the floor. I can assure you my feelings were not enviable at that moment. I had not even our old coolie with me, as he had succumbed to the fatigue of the long walk, and had remained in one of the villages we had passed through. Some people sitting about this resting-place, wishing, I suppose, to see what I was like, thrust one of the large coloured paper lanterns into the chair, and then laughed at my appearance.

I hoped to remain in this place until Henry's chair might arrive, but to my disappointment up I was taken after a delay of five minutes, and on we marched. You can imagine what my joy was when the steps of the other chair coolies became audible. When Henry came up, he told me that he had also felt very anxious about me. The coolies carrying his chair had become very much fatigued, and it was time for the other four to take their turn, but when inquired for, they were nowhere to be found. They had evidently given their friends the slip, and had slunk off in the dark. We arrived home about half-past nine, very tired, but having enjoyed the day's excursion most thoroughly.

Chapter 7 – Chimelong Safari Park

The Chimelong Safari Park

How to get there: Take metro line 3 to Hanxi Changlong station exit A. Follow signs over the pedestrian overpass. Take the free shuttle or walk to the entrance.

How much: 250 RMB Monday – Thursday, 280 RMB Friday – Sunday and holidays including school summer vacation. Discounts are available if visitors chose to visit more than one park.

How long: Full Day

Chimelong Park is part of a franchise spread across southern China. Guangzhou's Chimelong Safari Park is one part of the local complex and is part zoo and part open-land safari area with a focus on breeding and teaching. The white Siberian tiger, koala bear and panda populations have all been increased due to the efforts of the park. The full Chimelong complex in Guangzhou features a water park with slides and lazy river, an amusement park, the International Circus park which highlights acts similar to Cirque de Sol and the crocodile park focused on exotic wetland animals and birds.

Visitors to these parks stream out of the metro station with their bags of sunscreen and bathing suits. The directions to the parks are on a sign held by a cardboard, cartoon white tiger in a safari hat. It's the Chimelong mascot. Among the families and others spending the day at the parks is Tracy. She has short, dark brown hair and a round face with oval glasses. Her last visit to this park was seven years ago with her now ex-boyfriend. Today she appears chagrin. She lives only a few metro stops away but she got on the wrong train and went north instead of south; it took her an hour to get back. She's looking forward to seeing the lions, tigers and the other hunters – her favorites.

Guests walk up the metal stairs and over the pedestrian bridge to the shuttle bus terminal and parking lot. The safari park is the first drop-off point for visitors on the shuttle loop. Though they leave every five to ten minutes, the lines for these full-size buses can be long. A nearby sign says it only takes five to ten minutes to walk to the park and points the way.

Tracy is mopping her forehead with a tissue and wishing she had chosen the bus instead of trusting the signs. "It said it was a eight minute walk, and I think it was fifteen minutes to get here," she complains. The walk passes the amusement park and water park. Each park is playing the same cheerful song over the speakers, the theme music to one of China's most popular children's shows "Where's Father?" It's filmed in the parks explains Tracy. The soundtrack plays non-stop from hidden speakers. Most of the crowd chooses to spend time in the water and amusement parks. Those parks can get very crowded during weekends and holidays. The safari park is usually not crowded and the lay-out helps guests spread out.

The park was opened in 1997 and is a wild animal sanctuary and educational facility. Though parts of the Chimelong franchise have opened in other cities, only Guangzhou has a safari park[1]. It meets international standards for zoos and works in partnership with several breeding programs including an Australian koala bear program. Over five hundred species and twenty thousand animals live in the enclosures and free range park[2].

The north entrance is next to the parking lot, while the shuttle and walk lead visitors to the south gate. Before entering, many families stop at the "lunch check room." They bring a fully packed lunch in a large bag and leave it at the park entrance for pick-up later. Snack and lunch counters are available in the park, but they can be pricey. Inside, trees and dense shrubs shield one area from another. Once inside visitors follow the path created by the greenery around the flamingo pool.

Tracy jokes about the colors of the birds in this pond. "Flamingo. Probably they are white because they are in Guangzhou and this kind of white bird, they don't like to eat the spicy food. They drink milk and then they are just white. And for the red one, they eat spice food a lot. They like Szechuan food and they got burned, because it's too spicy," she says. After a moment she smiles and admits, "The reason is their food turns them red."

The park is divided into sections based on the homelands of the animals or the type of animals. The south entrance divides in two directions. The eastern path leads to the African exhibits of monkeys and lemurs. The western path is home to the elephants, giraffes, and panda bears. North of both paths are the tigers and the swan lake[3]. Each of the special animal areas, like the pandas, are separated from the main walkway. This helps the park direct the flow of visitors. It also ensures visitors pass through the gift shops that divide one section from another. Stuffed animals, key chains and t-shirts fill these shops.

Leaving the flamingos' pool, the path moves guests

straight towards the chimpanzee enclosure. Most of the enclosures are set up on an island system. For the chimpanzees, this means an open island fitted with trees, vines and swinging toys surrounded by water with a raised fence in the middle to prevent them from crossing. The trees branches are kept trimmed so chimps can't swing over the water. "I think they really feel like home, because it's hot enough here. Around 40° C [104° F]," Tracy says but, "I'm sure I'm exaggerating." There are smaller indoor enclosure spaces built for cold weather periods.

During the week, when the crowds are thinner, handlers bring some of the baby animals out to meet the guests. Visitors are not allowed to handle the animals, but can get a more up-close and personal experience. Photo stations with baby tigers and lions are set up around the park even on the busiest days. The cubs are kept in an indoor, air-conditioned play area separated from visitors by a child-high white picket fence. For 20 RMB guests can enter the play area to have their photo taken next to a cub. The money from these photo sessions is used to support the breeding programs and wildlife protection efforts[4].

Music from the nearby Hippo Theater draws a crowd to one of the several animal shows. There are three active animal theaters around the park: Hippo Theater, HuaGuoShan Theater (monkey and ape theater), and the Elephant Show[5]. At the south end of the park is also the White Tiger Theater. In the past, the big cats of the park would be brought into the fenced-off ring to balance on large balls, jump through hoops and pose after making long leaps from one platform to another. Currently, this theater is out of service and may not open again[6].

In the Hippo Theater all the seats are taken as the show begins. Late-comers stand on the stairs to watch the show.

Giant vultures swoop into the open field below. There are three entrances in the trees at the back of amphitheater that allow the animals and their handlers easy access to the field. A tall, bare tree stands in the center of the ring with sturdy branches for the birds of prey. Hawks and eagles spread their wings over the crowd as they glide toward perches built into the sides of the theater. It's an open air theater with a high canopy for the visitors sitting in the stands.

After the birds, the namesake of the theater trundles out. A single hippo is guided towards the large placement in the center of the ring. It is given a watermelon by its trainers and crushes it easily between powerful jaws. A young chimpanzee slaps his hands together above his head. The crowd follows the cue and begins to clap. The hippo and chimp are replaced by a small blackbird – the local myna. "He can read a poem, a Chinese poem," says Tracy about the little black bird who was her favorite.

The HuanGuoShan Theater, which is nearby, offers a monkey and ape show. These shows have the animals entering the open field with their trainer and following simple commands. They receive food treats and the commands are the type that trainers need to reinforce daily: "open your mouth" "hold out your foot." The commands are used by the trainers during routine medical checks. Because of the closeness, the theaters operate on a rotating schedule[7][8]. This prevents too many visitors returning to the main walkway at the same time.

After leaving the hippo show Tracy stops to watch two families of meerkats play. "It's cute, but I would rather not call them cats. They look like mice. How about meermouse," she suggests. They are the central figures of the courtyard and restaurant outside the hippo theater. From the courtyard it's easy for visitors to turn south towards the western path or continue on the eastern path towards the lemurs. The western path leads to the elephant enclosure, past the horse park and children's park and is the way Tracy chooses[9]. The children's park is a small amusement park with trains that go round in circles and tiny roller coasters which move on gentle slopes. These are common in parks all over China.

Turning onto the western path brings guest to the "elephant rides" sign. For a fee, visitors can climb the wooden platform to ride in the seat on the back of an Asian elephant. Its trainer leads the elephant in a circle. "Here you can just watch it, but you cannot touch it. It's not that fun," Tracy says. "In Thailand, you can just ride the elephant and have a tour in the forest and that's real fun." Next to the riding station is a watering hole and a dusty plain where the rest of the herd spend most of their time.

A trainer is selling bananas for visitors to throw across the divide to the elephants. This herd consists of several adults and a few adolescents. Their trunks stretch out to grab the bananas tossed across the 8 ft. (2.45m) gulch that divides their enclosure from the park. "It's fun feeding the elephants, but I'm just wondering if they are getting tired of eating bananas all the time," says Tracy.

These elephants are lucky. They are protected. China has a major problem with ivory traders. It is the world's largest consumer of ivory, and the legal market is dwarfed by the illegal one. On January 6, 2014 six tons of ivory carvings and tusks, worth over $10 million USD, were crushed in Dongguan, Guaungdong as part of a crackdown on the trade[10].

"Surveys conducted in China indicate that a large percentage of the Chinese public is not aware of the elephant poaching crisis in Africa and do not connect buying ivory with this crisis," says African Wildlife Foundation spokesperson Kathleen Garrigan. Basketball superstar, Yao Ming works to make the public more aware of the trouble. A photograph he shared of himself being followed by a baby elephant – whose entire family had been slaughtered – went viral in 2013. He wrote in his blog that Kinango the baby died shortly after the photo was taken. Yao attributed it to heartbreak. It's, "too common for the very young to lose their will to live after their mother and sometimes whole herd have been brutally taken from them," he wrote[11].

The elephants in Chimelong are Asian, not African. They are included in the park as part of the educational function of the park[12]. Elephant Theater connects to the enclosure. During the show the trainers work to make the visitors aware of the problems faced by elephants around the world. The WildAid survey found that most Chinese people, "think ivory comes from natural death. They didn't have a chance to have the correct information." Once the problem is explained to them ninety-five percent believed that ivory should be banned. The majority of ivory purchases come from Guangdong, Shaanxi, and Zhejiang provinces because, "that's where the most wealth is located," says May Mei, Chief Representative of WildAid China[13].

Northeast of the elephant exhibit is the entrance to the giant panda bear exhibit. Visitors follow the small side path to the panda house. The pandas live inside a long building with dividers between the habitats. "It's like a five star hotel here," says Tracy. "A well-protected animal, the most famous one in China, they are going extinct so they need to be protected," she says. Visitors usually find them asleep or eating, often turned away from the glass divider. Sleeping for most of the day is a trait shared with the koalas. Both eat a plant which is difficult to digest, so they spend most of their energy processing their food[8]. The pandas have climbing platforms and fresh bamboo in each enclosure. Each area also has an ice block on the floor. On hot days the pandas sprawl over the ice in a manner that sensitive guests might find alarming. They are not native to the low Guangdong forests, preferring high, cool mountains[14].

Pandas living in captivity is not new. Records suggest they were present in the Zhou court (1046 - 256 B.C.E.) and that even the legendary Yellow Emperor, Huangdi had one. The first example of "panda diplomacy" occurred in 685 C.E. when Empress Wu Zetian sent a pair of pandas to Japan[15]. An American heiress, Ruth Elizabeth Harkness, spent her own fortune to bring the first panda to the United States. Her first attempt in 1936 resulted in the capture of the infant male "Su Lin" who was raised in the Chicago zoo until his death two years later. His body is now on display in the Field Museum of Natural History[16][17].

"We don't need to pay extra money to see pandas, because they are everywhere in China. But in other countries, while I was traveling in Thailand or in Singapore in other countries, you need to pay extra money to see the pandas," Tracy says. She's leaning on the fiberglass barrier designed to look like yellow bamboo. "Panda diplomacy" was revived in the 1950's by the Chinese government.

Currently pandas are leased to other countries for ten-year periods at $1 million USD per year. Half of the lease fee is meant for conservation efforts for the wild panda population of 1,600 and their habitat. All pandas remain the property of China including any babies born abroad. Receiving a lease contract for a panda is generally part of a successful diplomatic mission, used as a sign of "national friendship[18]."

The end of the adult panda gallery leads into the Chimelong Panda School. The panda babies and mothers are cared for here. Panda pregnancy and birthing is a delicate process[19]. The first half of the building is dedicated to care and includes the veterinary services area. Visitors may pay to help mix the special "panda cakes" fed to the pandas at set times.

The second half of the building is where panda cubs are raised. Each group of cubs is placed in an enclosure with at least one other cub for company and toys, like plastic rocking horses.

Last stop for visitors on the panda path is the panda restaurant. The most expensive in the park, it's a sit-down restaurant with a large open window which looks out on a panda play area. Usually, an adult panda is in the enclosure. Customers can watch it play while eating. The restaurant exit puts visitors back at the south end of the park.

Taking the west path and passing the elephants again, guests find the Koala Restaurant Courtyard. Visitors can have lunch or a snack in the cafeteria-style restaurant. Five order stations serve fried rice, noodles and dumplings as part of their menu. The western path continues from here towards the koala exhibit.

A circular path into the koala area leaves the main road and brings visitors into the Australian animal section. In 2001, the park received six koalas from the Currumbin Wildlife Sanctuary as part of an international breeding program. Chimelong was the first park in mainland China to display koalas to the public. The program has been successful and there are now over twenty koalas at the park[20]. They each have an area with several eucalyptus trees to climb and sleep in. "They're really cute, but watching koalas is really boring. They just stay there, in the same position the whole day," says Tracy. She's shocked when one wakes up long enough to move to another branch.

The rest of the Australian area features wallabies and kangaroos. They lounge in the dusty, tall grass of their enclosures avoiding the afternoon heat. A few native bird species fill out the end of the loop. A petting station encourages visitors to pet an iguana resting on a tree branch before returning to the main road. Tracy gives it a try, but finds the skin of the large lizard a bit too weird. "It's gross," she says.

Across the main road is the giraffe feeding and viewing station. A trainer sells leafy branches for 5 RMB. A man buys some for his daughter and lifts her up so she can hold out the branches, but she refuses to stretch out her arm. "They are cute and weird, and actually they are lovely, but smelly," says Tracy. Her own branches were taken by a long, dark purple giraffe tongue a few minutes ago. The viewing platform is raised so the giraffes' heads are level with guests. This small portion of the herd stands in a paddock the size of a football field. An opening at the back allows them to walk into the free range section of the park. When they tire of eating hand-picked greenery they wander away.

North of the giraffes and koalas is the side path that leads to the big cats. Every half hour music fills the area announcing the tigers "diving show." "They're feeding the white tigers, and they use the meat to lure the tigers to jump into the water," says Tracy adding, "I want to dive, too." The solid glass walls divide the visitors from the water that surrounds the adolescent white tigers' area. Wooden posts the size of telephone poles are set into the ground in the center of the enclosure. Metal wires at the tops act like laundry lines. Trainers attach chunks of meat to clips which slide out on the lines. The tigers choose to jump for the meat. They grab the meat in their teeth and drop into the water near the glass. Paddling in the cool water, they don't always choose to exit quickly. These are adolescent tigers, brothers and cousins, who have grown-up together[21].

The other tigers are in standard zoo-sized enclosures. They are members of various tiger species, all of which are endangered. The park's most successful breeding program is found here. The largest enclosure, which stretches at least an acre and has several stone hills and man-made caves, is the home of Kelly and her family. She is a white tiger and the founder of a 150-member family. Her and her descendants account for roughly half of the total quantity of white tigers in the world[22].

"We tried to feed the tigers. We threw a lot of meat: chicken, pork. We have a lot of tries, but still we can't draw their attention successfully," says Tracy. She bought a small package of raw meat from a trainer and threw it like a baseball into the enclosure. The tiger sitting on a nearby rock was not impressed enough to get up from its nap. "They're tired of meat already. Chicken. They want something, emu, something different," she says to explain the bored reaction from the tigers.

The successful breeding of Bengal tigers, golden tigers and snow tigers has encouraged the park to try with the South China tiger – one of the ten most endangered animals in the world. The population has dwindled to a few dozen due to habitat loss in the southern China region. Today they exist in the wild in only three small mountain regions. The park received two South China tigers in 2010 and is researching breeding practices before starting the new program[23].

Cliff paintings from the Stone age and the golden tiger passport found in the Nanyue King's tomb show the respect people have always had for these animals. The tiger is "the king of beasts" in China. It came to represent military courage and strength. As an animal of power, tigers were gods of the mountains. The natural match to dragons in the waters. They protected against fire, theft and evil. Images were often carved on doors or hung in entryways as prevention against thieves and vengeful spirits. Unfortunately, they are poached for their teeth, claws and skins and their natural habitats are logged so heavily most of it is now gone[24][25].

Visitors leave the tiger area and cross the road to the Animal Kindergarten. Here tiger and lion cubs are raised before introduction to the adult population or being sent to other breeding programs. The building is filled with fluffy cubs the size of small dogs. They roll and tumble in play or nap in exhausted heaps. The outdoor enclosure is filled with logs and climbing areas, a tiger jungle gym. "It's their kindergarten here and they are playing the game inside. Just now we saw four, but suddenly we can only find three. I guess they are playing hide-and-seek," Tracy says. The cubs spend their first two years in the kindergarten before moving to the diving enclosure. They stay with their cousins and siblings to reduce conflicts and increase their mental and physical health[26].

Leaving the kindergarten, visitors find themselves across from the large lake filled with a variety of swans and other non-native water fowl. This is a good place for a rest and many guests take advantage of the sheltered benches and cool breezes found here. Behind them is a courtyard with a choice: dinosaurs or the wheeled safari. The dinosaur path leads to several motorized versions of dinosaurs living in the fog of the past. At the end of the path a cave contains an angry tyrannosaurus looming over visitors. It seems to be attacking a spinosaurus. Some visitors find themselves a bit damp after the T-rex "sneezes" cold mist at them.

The other choice leads to the loading area for the wheeled trains. Visitors are driven into the free range section of the park that the animals wander over together. "A lot of different animals from a lot of different parts of the world," says Tracy. "We kind of slowly drive through different areas." The train weaves through the areas so visitors get the best possible views. Animals which won't peacefully coexist, like the leopards and lions, are separated from the others by deep gulches and high fences. The trip lasts about forty minutes.

The wheeled train returns visitors to the courtyard, making it easy for them to enter the dinosaur path. Near closing time visitors move towards the exits. Tracy joins the shuffle towards the southern gate. The shuttle stop is now the last pickup of the run. Buses are full as everyone leaves and many choose to walk in the cooler evening air. "The park is bigger than what I thought," Tracy says. She noticed that the park has been expanded since she was here seven years ago. "It really took one day and you should spend more time here. It's great, fantastic."

Mrs. John Henry Gray to her mother excerpted from her book *Fourteen Months in Canton* published in 1880 and is now in the public domain.

Letter XXXIX -

Canton, April 10th, 1878
My dear Mother,

    The day before yesterday we went into the city and reinspected many branches of Chinese industry. I was much interested in my visit to the dye-works, where I saw the process of dyeing cotton clothes, and had it fully explained to me. In the inner division of the factory, several large vats stood filled with blue dye for printing the blue cotton so much used by the Chinese, or with a prune-coloured dye also used for dyeing cotton stuffs. The blue dye is composed of indigo, water, native wine, and lirae.

    The prune dye is produced by tanning bark, which is brought in large quantities from Siam [Thailand]. The process of dyeing these cloths is repeated fourteen times, if the colour is to be a dark blue, but four times only, if the colour is to be a light shade of blue. The cotton cloth is then ready to be calendered. I was much amused in watching the primitive means used by the workmen to moisten the fabric before placing it under the stone rollers which are used by the calenderers. They take mouthfuls of water from the spouts of teapots, and then squirt the water from their mouths over the cloth. It is astonishing how much water these men, by practice, can take into their mouths at one time. The calendaring is performed by men standing on large granite stones, which they move up and down by their naked feet, the cotton cloth being placed on wooden rollers underneath these stones.

On leaving the dye-works we went on to a tobacco manufactory. Here we saw women employed in the upper rooms of the factory, in picking the fibres from the tobacco leaves. They worked most rapidly, and did not leave off as they gazed in surprise upon us. Below, men were engaged in spreading the leaves, which had been prepared by the women, on a wooden platform and trampling them under their naked feet. They sprinkled the leaves occasionally with oil, and then threw a red-coloured powder over them to give them a red colour. The tobacco leaves were then gathered together, and pressed by means of flat boards placed under a large wooden beam. This pressure reduces them into the form of large cakes.

Workmen were employed in another part of the factory in cutting these compressed leaves into small particles, and others were weighing certain quantities, and making them up into packets. These packets were then place in ovens, heated by charcoal, for the purpose of being dried. On being removed from the ovens they were ready to be sold wholesale or retail to customers.

In passing through Cheung-Lok street, we entered some small shops to inspect specimens of wood-carving. Some which were richly carved were intended for temple decorations or for the ornamentation of private houses. The devices in many instances were very strange. The street occupied by lapidaries, who are engaged in cutting jadestone, was the next place at which we made a halt. We went into three or four of these workshops, and I was much amused by the cool manner in which Henry took out jadestone thumb-rings, bracelets, or whatever was in the machines, and showed them to me. The workmen laughed and nodded, and, knowing Henry so well from his constant visits to their workshops, they stopped or went on with their work as he directed.

The cutting of the large blocks of jadestone is done by

means of wire saws, which are made in the form of bows having strings of plaited steel wire. The sawyers stand on each side of the block of jadestone, and pull the wire saw backwards and forwards in a horizontal direction. They drop emery powder mixed with water on the part of the stone they are cutting. When the blocks of jadestone have been divided into pieces, they are handed on to other lapidaries who form them into ornaments by small circular saws. The jadestone varies much in colour, from white to light and dark green.

Having watched the lapidaries for some time, we went on to the Ch'uung-Shau-Tsze, a monastery in which the Buddha of longevity is worshipped. He is represented, as a very fat, merry-looking old man. Portraits of him are often to be seen in shops where pictures are sold, and little bronze and porcelain images of him are for sale in the curiosity shops.

There is a pretty landscape garden attached to this monastery, and, in a nursery garden belonging to it, we saw large earthen-ware vessels filled with gold fish. There were square troughs containing many of these brilliant creatures in all stages of growth, from spawn up to the fully-grown fish. This Chinese golden carp has a very long tail divided in the centre, with two drooping fans on each side. Its eyes are peculiarly prominent. It is indigenous to the country. We afterwards inspected some carvings in mother-of-pearl, which were beautifully executed. The carving is deep and rich. This is surprising, as the instruments used by the workmen are of a most primitive kind.

We also visited some of the shops where silk-weaving was going on. As you enter the Chow Ch'uung-Tuung street, you hear the sound of shuttles being thrown rapidly from one side of the looms to the other. This street is the very centre of the silk-weaving district of the city of Canton. The loom used for plain weaving differs little from that which is employed in

England, but the frames in use here for fancy silks are most dissimilar to those used in England for the same purpose, and are most primitive in form. The draw-boy sits above the frame, and pulls the strings by which he brings down the warp-thread through which the shuttle has to pass to form the pattern, I saw many beautiful webs of silk being made, and I was struck by some of the colours, which were lovely in shade.

We were now quite close to one of the water streets. I do not remember whether I have described these water lanes to you, in a former letter. They are most curious, and remind all European travelers of the water streets of Venice, only here you have no palaces, but ordinary houses on each side of them. As I stood in an open doorway, looking down one of these water streets, namely that which is called, in Chinese, Sai-hoi, I could imagine that there must be a great resemblance. The inhabitants of the houses step out of their doors into boats, when they want to go from their homes. A very large water-gate, through which boats pass within and without the walls of the city, stands at the end of this water street.

Leaving this place, we went through the street called Chong-Uen-Fong, famous for its beautiful embroidery. We entered into many of the open shops where men and boys were working beautiful patterns on silk or satin in frames. I saw most lovely pieces of embroidery in hand, some of which were intended for large ancestral, or longevity banners, and others as coverings for altars. In some cases the embroidery was for mandarins' dresses or ladies' tunics.

The shading of colours was most charming, and I thought the flowers and butterflies introduced into the patterns were exquisitely worked. The pattern is sketched in white chalk, on the silk or satin before the embroidery is begun. I am much in love with this rich work, and also with the beautiful fringes made by the Chinese. The embroidery varies very much in quality, a fact you do not observe so much at first, but as the eye becomes educated, you can detect the different qualities at once.

We paid a most interesting visit to the shop of a gold-beater in this street. In this shop two men were beating out gold into extremely fine sheets. The gold was placed between pieces of black paper, and several of them being so arranged, they were covered over with thick white pasteboard, then placed on a block of unpolished marble. The men who sat on each side of the block proceeded to beat the packets of gold with extremely heavy hammers, and whilst they were so employed streams of perspiration fell from their naked shoulders.

I was amused at seeing two boys who stood behind these workmen, and fanned them without ceasing. Some shops in this neighbourhood, in which horn lanterns are made and exposed for sale, much pleased me. I wish you could see these lanterns, which are manufactured by a singular process, and are made in most varied shapes and sizes. Many of them are beautifully painted, and framed in black carved wood.

I cannot tell you all I saw in these interesting streets, but I may mention the work in kingfisher's feathers which we examined, and the beautiful feather fans made from the plumage of many a lovely bird. As fans are such necessary articles for use in this country, the supply is most varied, and the prices asked for them ranges from a few cash to many dollars.

The carving in ivory too, by means of very primitive instruments, came under our notice. I saw an elephant's tusk which was being exquisitely carved. It had been some months under the workman's hands, and was still far from completion. It was to be offered for sale at a very high price.

We now felt in need of some refreshment, and therefore

went into a large tea-saloon. I was very tired with my morning's work, but I had enjoyed it most thoroughly. It was intensely interesting to see the industries which are carried on at the present moment in this country in a precisely similar manner as they were in ages past, and I felt while inspecting them as if I had been removed into centuries long since gone by. And now I must give you a description of the tea-saloon into which we entered in search of refreshments.

It, as a rule with all these tea-saloons, of which there are very many in Canton, consists of two of three storeys, in each of which small tables are placed with chairs arranged around them. These saloons are very grand, being richly ornamented with carved wood-work, and all the arrangements in them are beautifully clean. In fact they are infinitely superior in all particulars to public-houses in Europe, the place of which they supply in China.

There is a furnace in each storey which supplies boiling water for the tea, the only beverage consumed in these saloons. On taking our seats in the upper room, round one of the small tables, a lacquerware box, divided into compartments and containing cakes of various kinds and many preserved fruits, was placed before us; cups of tea, too, were handed to us. You cannot help being struck with the republican spirit which is shown in this conservative country in many particulars. In these saloons rich and poor occupy the same room; a man in silk at one table, a man in cotton clothes at another. In Canton you do not see any Chinese women in these saloons.

We much enjoyed our tea-cakes, preserved cherries, ginger, plums, and kum-kwats. When we had finished our repast, we called one of the waiting men to us, for the purpose of paying our bill. And now I saw the method they adopt for charging. The waiter took up the lacquerware box, and counted how many cakes and fruits remained in it, he knowing the number of each which it contained previous to its having been placed before us.

As we were passing out of the room, this waiter called out of the room the sura we were indebted, to an accountant, who sat behind a little counter at the door. And here we paid a trifling sum, so it seemed to me, for our luncheon. On going downstairs Henry took me into the large kitchen, at the back of the building, where several cooks were occupied in making cakes of different kinds, and from the piles and piles of little cakes just ready for use, one felt how much these places of refreshment must be resorted to by the Chinese.

How incalculable would be the advantages to the English people, if similar refreshment-rooms were established in England, where neither wine nor spirits would tempt the poor man to drink away his hardly-earned wages. When we arrived at the door of the tea-saloon, we found the street was much crowded, and, on asking the reason, were told that the procession of Paak-tai was about to pass down the street. We, therefore, took up our station at the door of the tea-saloon to see it go by.

As you will be sure to remember my long description of a similar procession last year, I need not say much about this one, only that it differed in some particulars from the first I had seen. It was not on so large a scale, but the umbrellas, banners, etc., carried in it were new, and consequently very bright. One of its features I had not observed in the procession of last year. Various scenes were represented by children and young people, who were grouped on portable platforms.

I saw, in one of these set pieces, a fortune-teller represented, with a lady consulting him. In another two ladies were playing cards. In one group the actors (children) were seated in a boat. A garden scene, with a group of people sitting in it, was prettily arranged. The girls composing some of these groups were immensely rouged, and wore beautifully embroidered silk costumes. The little boys wore beards, or long moustaches, and slanting eyebrows were gummed on to their foreheads.

After the procession had passed, we paid a hurried visit to the Kwoh-Laan, or fruit market. In this market, which is one of the great extent, there is for sale, at all seasons of the year, an almost countless variety of fruits. Of the fruits which, at stated times, are here exposed for sale, we may enumerate the orange, citron, pumniolo, apple, rose-apple, custard-apple, pine-apple, pear, carambola, quince, guava, loquat, pomegranate, pumpkin, plantain, apricot, peach, plum, persimmon, grape, mango, melon, mulberry, lichi, wampee, date, luung-ngaan, arbutus, olive, cocoa-nut, walnut, chestnut, water-chestnut, and pea-nut. There is always a great variety of fruit exposed for sale in this, the Covent Garden of Canton, and I often pass through it to see the fruits, many of which are strange to me.

We had a very enjoyable excursion yesterday, some little way up the Fa-ti creek, our intention in starting being to go to a literary pagoda at Nam-Cheang and to take our afternoon tea at the foot of it. But first we paid, in passing, a visit to two or three of the gardens at Fa-ti. It is always a pleasure to me to stroll through these curious gardens. The first impression of them has naturally worn off, but their singularity strikes me afresh each time I enter them. It would be impossible to bring them as they are before your imagination, as you have seen nothing of the kind in England.

I will try, however, to give you a short description of them. In the first place, the Chinese do not grow their flowers in beds, nor let them spread from one to the other as we do. They grow all their flowers in pots. Rows of them line the paths in these gardens, and I have seen lovely shows of them, including roses, cockscombs, camellias, magnolias, chrysanthema, rhododendrons, balsams, azaleas, the narcissus, lotus, etc.

As I have walked up and down these gardens again and again, I have been amused at seeing numbers and numbers of plants trained over wire shapes into various devices, such as deer, serpents, dolphins, pagodas, birds, fans, boats, flower-baskets, and lastly, and by far the most noticeable and numerous, those which are made to represent Englishmen. The latter are most grotesque. The body, down to the knees, is made in a wire shape with the plant trained and cut over it, marking out the outline. A tall hat covers a composition head, which is invariable represented with red hair and whiskers. High black boots are added below the knees, and composition hands holding a stick complete these strange figures.

Sometimes earthenware dogs are represented at the heels of these caricatures. Cantonese dogs never follow their masters, they are not trained to do so, but are regarded as watch-dogs only. It therefore strikes the Chinese in this city as most curious to see Europeans followed by their dogs. A stick, too, is not allowed to be used in China, by any man under seventy years of age, and it is then used as a staff. And so again the habit of able-bodied Europeans carrying walking-sticks is very strange to the eyes of the Cantonese.

The dwarf-trees, grown in pots, which these gardens contain in great abundance, are very singular. Some of them, especially the pear-trees, are of great age, and are not more than from one to two feet high. Many have all the appearance of gnarled oaks in miniature. I do not think, however, they are so wonderful as the dwarf-trees which I saw in Japan. The latter appeared to me as possessing more twisted branches, and as being more compressed in form that those to be found in the Fa-ti gardens.

We now re-entered our sampan and went on to Nam-Cheang. The literary pagoda, at the foot of which we took our seats, is a graceful structure and charmingly decorated with porcelain frescoes. The tea was brought to us by our coolie from the boat, boiling water was soon got ready over a little fire of sticks, and we sipped our tea and gazed upon the strange country in front of us.

Having finished our tea we went into a small and dirty temple dedicated to the gods of learning. Such frightful idols they were, with a hideous attendant in effigy standing on each side of the chief altar. We then took a stroll through the small village, followed, as we usually are when passing through country villages, by boys and girls, the latter being very considerably in the minority. The girls, without exception, wore their hair cut in a fringe across their foreheads, and I knew from this that they were not only unmarried, but unaffianced. A young Chinese girl wears her back hair in a single plait hanging over her shoulders, the front hair is brought over the forehead, but as soon as she is betrothed, the fringe is brushed back and the back hair is dressed in a hi teapot.

Followed by an admiring throng of village children, we walked on a little way from Nam-Cheang to inspect a large granite arch raised in honour of Lau-laong-Shee, a woman who attained to the great age of a hundred years, and who in consequence received this posthumous honour. The arch is high, and two figures are carved in relief on it, which represent old age. Characters, engraved on it, purport that it is raised by imperial decree, and give the name of the lady thus honoured. This arch was raised some forty years ago.

We were so much vexed the other day, on coming home from one of our excursions, to find that a party of ten Chinese ladies had called upon us. I wish they had given us notice of their intended visit, as I should have liked so much to entertain them, and certainly should have stayed at home to receive them.

- Editor's Note: Mrs. Gray dated her last letter May 4th, 1878. In it she describes being invited to witness the installment of a new Buddhist abbot at a local temple. Soon after this final letter was sent, she and her family left Guangzhou for England. When she returned to her home country she collected the letters together and published them in London with printers William Clowes and Sons based in Stamford Street and publisher Macmillan and Co. in 1880. She dedicate the work to her husband, "whose long residence in the city of Canton, and intimate acquaintance with its inhabitants, enabled me to see and learn so much of their manners and customs." Most copies of her original published work are now found in rare book collections, but at least one was scanned and is available for free download in eReader formats. It has also been reprinted by various publishers.

Bard

Works Cited and References

Maps –

1. Cartographic Publishing House of Guangdong Province. "Guangzhou Map." Street map. Guangzhou, China and surrounding cities: Cartographic Publishing House of Guangdong Province, May 2012
2. Chinatechnews.com. "Map of Guangzhou." Street Map. Guangzhou, China: Chinatechnews.com, 2013. http://www.chinatechnews.com/wp-content/uploads/guangzhou-chinese-map.gif.
3. Drooman, Rev. D. "Map of the City and Entire Suburb's of Canton." Street Map. Guangzhou, China, 1860. http://upload.wikimedia.org/wikipedia/commons/d/da/Canton1860.jpg.
4. Maps Press of Guangdong Province. "Guangzhou: Tourist map of Guangzhou." Street map. Guangzhou, China: Maps Press of Guangdong Province, Januage 1, 2009
5. "Plan of the City of Canton." Street Map. Guangzhou, China, 1910. http://upload.wikimedia.org/wikipedia/commons/3/33/Plan_of_Canton.jpg.

Introduction –

1. Faure, David. *Emperor and Ancestory: State and Lineage in South China*. 1st ed. Stanford, California: Stanford University Press, 2007.
2. National Geographic. *National Geographic Atlas of China: An Expansive Portrait of China Today with More than 400 Maps and Illustrations*. 1st ed. Washington D.C.: National Geographic, 2007.
3. Brinkhoff, T. "The Principal Agglomerations of the World – Population Statistics & Maps." Citypopulation.de, April 5, 2011.
4. Gray, John Henry Mrs. *Fourteen Months in Canton*. London: Macmillan and Co., 1880. http://catalog.hathitrust.org/Record/006122760.
5. Rand McNally *Illustrated Atlas of China*. Rand McNally, 1972.
6. "Zhongguo Gujin Diming Dacidian 中国古今地名大词典," 2005, 2901.
7. Faure, *Emperor and Ancestory*, 1-464
8. Gray, *Fourteen Months in Canton*, 1-444

Chapter 1 – Chen Clan Academy

1. Gray, Mrs. John Henry. *Fourteen Months in Canton*. London: Macmillan and Co., 1880. http://catalog.hathitrust.org/Record/006122760.
2. "Informational Signs: Signs at the Site Provided Facts and Details Which Were Useful in the Understanding of the Size and History of the Site," n.d.
3. Guangdong Folk Art Museum PR Staff. "Guangdong Folk Art Museum Brochure," 2013.

4. Faure, David. *Emperor and Ancestory: State and Lineage in South China*. 1st ed. Stanford, California: Stanford University Press, 2007.
5. "Informational Signs"
6. Faure, *Emperor and Ancestory*, 1-464
7. ibid.
8. Gray, *Fourteen Months in Canton*, 1-444
9. Faure, *Emperor and Ancestory*, 1-464
10. Gray, *Fourteen Months in Canton*, 1-444
11. Faure, *Emperor and Ancestory*, 1-464
12. "Informational Signs"
13. Maps Press of Guangdong Province. "Guangzhou: Tourist Map of Guangzhou." Street map. Guangzhou, China: Maps Press of Guangdong Province, January 1, 2009.
14. Guangdong Folk Art Museum PR Staff. "Guangdong Folk Arts Museum ticket," 2013.
15. "Guangdong Folk Art Museum Brochure"
16. Stewart, Chris. Gong Xi Fa Cai! Audio. The History of China. Accessed February 2, 2014. www.thehistoryofchina.wordpress.com/.
17. "Informational Signs"
18. "Guangdong Folk Art Museum Brochure"
19. Guangzhen, Zhou, and Lu Tseng Gunn. Chinese Ceramic Cultural Sites: A Traveler's Handbook. Edited by Deborah Bouchette. California: Polly Chang, Wushing Books Publ. Col. Ltd., 2004.
20. ibid.
21. Twitchett, Denis, and Michael Loewe, eds. *The Cambridge History of China: Vol.1 The Ch'in and Han Empires, 221 B.C. - A.D. 220*. 2nd ed. Vol. 1. 10 vols. Cambridge, England: Press Syndicate of the University of Cambridge, 1986.

22. "Informational Signs"
23. ibid.
24. ibid.
25. Guangzhen, <u>Chinese Ceramic Cultural Sites</u>, 159-164
26. "Informational Signs"
27. Faure, *Emperor and Ancestory*, 1-464
28. "Informational Signs"
29. ibid.
30. "Guangdong Folk Art Museum Brochure"
31. "Informational Signs"
32. Faure, *Emperor and Ancestory*, 1-464
33. Manuel, Dave. "Inflation Calculator." DaveManuel.com, 2014. www.davemanuel.com/inflation-calculator.php.
34. Gershtein, Sergey, and Anna Gershtein. "Tael (leung) Conversion Chart: Mass and Weight Conversions, Hong Kong," 2013. m.convert-me.com/en/convert/weight/hontael.html.

Chapter 2 – Guangdong Museum

1. Guangdong Museum. "Guangdong Museum." Guangzhou Museum PR department, 2013.
2. Guangdong Museum. "Visitors Guide." Guangzhou Museum PR department, 2013.
3. "Informational Signs: Signs at the Site Provided Facts and Details Which Were Useful in the Understanding of the Size and History of the Site," n.d.

4. Lambert, Katie, and Sara Dowdy. How the Opium Wars Worked. Audio. Stuff You Missed in History Class. Accessed November 14, 2009. www.missedinhistory.com/podcasts/how-the-opium-wars-worked.
5. "Informational Signs"
6. Stewart, Chris. Them Bones, Them Bones, Them Oracle Bones. Audio. The History of China. Accessed December 15, 2013. www.thehistoryofchina.wordpress.com.
7. Stewart, Chris. Live Fast, Die Young. Audio. The History of China. Accessed August 24, 2014. www.thehistoryofchina.wordpress.com.
8. Guangdong Museum. "Purple Stone: Exhibition of the Duan Inkstone through Dynasties." Guangzhou Museum PR department, 2013.
9. Stewart, Live Fast, Die Young, Audio
10. Guangdong Museum, "Purple Stone"
11. ibid.
12. Guangdong Museum. "Beauty Is Gilt Wood: Chaozhou Woodcarving Art Exhibition." Guangzhou Museum PR department, 2013.
13. Guangdong Museum, "Visitors Guide"
14. "Informational Signs"
15. Guangdong Museum, "Beauty Is Gilt Wood"
16. "Informational Signs"
17. Guangdong Museum, "Beauty Is Gilt Wood"
18. "Informational Signs"
19. Faure, David. *Emperor and Ancestory: State and Lineage in South China*. 1st ed. Stanford, California: Stanford University Press, 2007.
20. Guangdong Museum, "Beauty Is Gilt Wood"
21. "Informational Signs"

22. ibid.
23. Guangdong Museum. "Exhibition of Pottery and Porcelain through Dynasties." Guangzhou Museum PR department, 2013.
24. De Delftse Paux. "Delft Pottery De Delftse Pauw: History." De Delftse Paux, 2012. www.delftpottery.com/history.html.
25. Guangdong Museum, "Exhibition of Pottery and Porcelain…"
26. "Informational Signs"
27. Guangdong Museum, "Exhibition of Pottery and Porcelain…"
28. "Informational Signs"
29. Guangdong Museum. "Exhibition of Guangdong History and Culture." Guangzhou Museum PR department, 2013.
30. ibid.
31. "Informational Signs"
32. Faure, *Emperor and Ancestory*, 1-464
33. "Informational Signs"
34. Faure, *Emperor and Ancestory*, 1-464
35. Guangdong Museum, "Exhibition of Guangdong History…"
36. Guangdong Museum, "Visitors Guide"
37. "Informational Signs"
38. ibid.
39. Faure, *Emperor and Ancestory*, 1-464
40. ibid.
41. ibid.
42. "Informational Signs"
43. Faure, *Emperor and Ancestory*, 1-464
44. Guangdong Museum, "Exhibition of Guangdong History…"

45. "Informational Signs"
46. ibid.
47. TravelChinaGuide.com. "Dragon Boat Festival." TravelChinaGuide.com, 1998. Accessed April 10, 2014. www.travelchinaguide.com/essential/holidays/dragon-boat.htm.
48. ibid.
49. Faure, *Emperor and Ancestory*, 1-464
50. ibid.
51. "Informational Signs"
52. Faure, *Emperor and Ancestory*, 1-464
53. "Informational Signs"
54. Guangdong Museum, "Visitors Guide"
55. Guangdong Museum. "Guangdong Natural Resource Display." Guangzhou Museum PR department, 2013.
56. "Informational Signs"
57. Faure, *Emperor and Ancestory*, 1-464
58. Fasman, Jon. "Food for Thought: Taste for Rare, Wild Pangolin Is Driving the Mammal to Extinction." NPR.org. August 3, 2014.
59. Sedghi, Ami. "Which Cities Do the World's Millionaires and Billionaires Live In?" The Guardian. May 8, 2013, sec. News.
60. Foote, Mike. "Morphological Diversity in the Evolutionary Radition of Paleozoic and Post-Paleozoic Crinoids." Paleobiology 25, no. sp1 (1999): 1–116.
61. Gradstein, Felix M., J.G. Ogg, and A.G. Smith. <u>A Geologic Time Scale 2004</u>. Cambridge: Cambridge University Press, 2004.
62. Branigan, Tania. "Chinese 'Dinosaur City' Reshpaes Understanding of Prehistoric Era." The Guardian. May 13, 2011, Online edition, sec. Science.

63. Daily Mail Reporter. "'Dinosaur City': World's Largest Fossil Site Unearthed in China." Daily Mail: Mail Online. December 30, 2008, sec. Science.

Chapter 3 – Museum of the Nanyue King of the Western Han Dynasty

1. Shurong, Cai. "The Museum of the Nanyue King of Western Han Dynasty." The Museum of the Nanyue King of Western Han Dynasty PR department, 2013.
2. Cartographic Publishing House of Guangdong Province. "Guangzhou Map." Street Map. Guangzhou, China and surrounding cities: Cartographic Publishing House of Guangdong Province, May 2012.
3. Twitchett, Denis, and Michael Loewe, eds. *The Cambridge History of China: Vol.1 The Ch'in and Han Empires, 221 B.C. - A.D. 220.* 2nd ed. Vol. 1. 10 vols. Cambridge, England: Press Syndicate of the University of Cambridge, 1986.
4. "Informational Signs: Signs at the Site Provided Facts and Details Which Were Useful in the Understanding of the Size and History of the Site," n.d.
5. ibid.
6. ibid.
7. Faure, David. *Emperor and Ancestory: State and Lineage in South China.* 1st ed. Stanford, California: Stanford University Press, 2007.
8. Twitchett, *The Cambridge History of China*, 1-981
9. Faure, *Emperor and Ancestory*, 1-464

10. Stewart, Chris. <u>One Nation Under Qin</u>. Audio. The History of China. Accessed May 10, 2014. www.thehistoryofchina.wordpress.com.
11. Twitchett, *The Cambridge History of China*, 1-981
12. ibid.
13. "Informational Signs"
14. ibid.
15. ibid.
16. Shurong, "The Museum of the Nanyue King…"
17. "Informational Signs"
18. ibid.
19. Shurong, "The Museum of the Nanyue King…"
20. "Informational Signs"
21. ibid.
22. Shurong, "The Museum of the Nanyue King…"
23. Faure, *Emperor and Ancestory*, 1-464
24. "Informational Signs"
25. Shurong, "The Museum of the Nanyue King…"
26. "Informational Signs"
27. ibid.
28. ibid.
29. Cammann, Schuyler V.R. "A Rare 'Jade' Book: A Manchu Emperor's Edict Carved on Panels of Jade." Expedition, no. Spring 1980 (1980): 27–33.
30. "Informational Signs"
31. Shurong, "The Museum of the Nanyue King…"
32. "Informational Signs"
33. Shurong, "The Museum of the Nanyue King…"
34. Faure, *Emperor and Ancestory*, 1-464
35. "Informational Signs"
36. ibid.
37. ibid.
38. Shurong, "The Museum of the Nanyue King…"

39. Faure, *Emperor and Ancestory*, 1-464
40. "Informational Signs"
41. ibid.
42. Shurong, "The Museum of the Nanyue King..."
43. "Informational Signs"
44. ibid.
45. Guangzhen, Zhou, and Lu Tseng Gunn. <u>Chinese Ceramic Cultural Sites: A Traveler's Handbook</u>. Edited by Deborah Bouchette. California: Polly Chang, Wushing Books Publ. Col. Ltd., 2004.
46. "Informational Signs"
47. Shurong, "The Museum of the Nanyue King..."
48. "Informational Signs"
49. Faure, *Emperor and Ancestory*, 1-464
50. Stewart, Chris. <u>Every Direction But the Sea</u>. Audio. The History of China. Accessed July 7, 2014. www.thehistoryofchina.wordpress.com.
51. Twitchett, *The Cambridge History of China*, 1-981
52. Guangdong Museum. "Exhibition of Pottery and Porcelain through Dynasties." Guangzhou Museum PR department, 2013.

Chapter 4 – Temple District

1. Twitchett, Denis, and Michael Loewe, eds. *The Cambridge History of China: Vol.1 The Ch'in and Han Empires, 221 B.C. - A.D. 220.* 2nd ed. Vol. 1. 10 vols. Cambridge, England: Press Syndicate of the University of Cambridge, 1986.
2. "Guangxiao Temple ticket." 2013.

3. Maps Press of Guangdong Province. "Guangzhou: Tourist Map of Guangzhou." Street map. Guangzhou, China: Maps Press of Guangdong Province, January 1, 2009.
4. "You Gotta Have Faith: The Role of Religion in Modern China." That's PRD, January 2014.
5. Faure, David. *Emperor and Ancestory: State and Lineage in South China.* 1st ed. Stanford, California: Stanford University Press, 2007.
6. Twitchett, *The Cambridge History of China*, 1-981
7. That's PRD, "You Gotta Have Faith…"
8. "Informational Signs: Signs at the Site Provided Facts and Details Which Were Useful in the Understanding of the Size and History of the Site," n.d.
9. Faure, *Emperor and Ancestory*, 1-464
10. ibid.
11. "Guangxiao Temple ticket"
12. Faure, *Emperor and Ancestory*, 1-464
13. "Guangzhou Six Banyan Pagoda: Introduction to Liurong Temple." Guangzhou Six Banyan Pagoda PR department, 2013.
14. Faure, *Emperor and Ancestory*, 1-464
15. "Guangzhong Liurong Temple ticket." 2013.
16. "Informational Signs"
17. "Guangzhou Six Banyan Pagoda"
18. "Guangzhou Liurong Temple ticket"
19. "Guangzhou Six Banyan Pagoda"
20. "Informational Signs"
21. Maps Press of Guangdong Province. "Guangzhou: Tourist Map of Guangzhou."
22. "Informational Signs"
23. That's PRD, "You Gotta Have Faith…"
24. "Informational Signs"

25. ibid.
26. That's PRD, "You Gotta Have Faith…"
27. Faure, *Emperor and Ancestory*, 1-464
28. That's PRD, "You Gotta Have Faith…"
29. Faure, *Emperor and Ancestory*, 1-464
30. That's PRD, "You Gotta Have Faith…"
31. ibid.
32. "Informational Signs"
33. "Five-Immortal Temple: Museum of Yuexiu District Guangzhou pamphlet." Five-Immortal Temple PR department, 2013.
34. "Informational Signs"
35. Faure, *Emperor and Ancestory*, 1-464
36. "Informational Signs"
37. Faure, *Emperor and Ancestory*, 1-464
38. "Informational Signs"
39. Faure, *Emperor and Ancestory*, 1-464
40. "Informational Signs"
41. "Museum of Yuexiu District ticket." 2013.
42. Cody, David. "Dissenters." The Victorian Web, August 2002. Accessed April 12, 2015. www.victorianweb.org/religion/dissntrs.html

Chapter 5 – Yuexiu Park

1. Maps Press of Guangdong Province. "Guangzhou: Tourist Map of Guangzhou." Street map. Guangzhou, China: Maps Press of Guangdong Province, January 1, 2009.
2. "Informational Signs: Signs at the Site Provided Facts and Details Which Were Useful in the Understanding of the Size and History of the Site," n.d.

3. Maps Press of Guangdong Province. "Guangzhou: Tourist Map of Guangzhou."
4. The People's Government of Guangzhou Municipality. "Guangzhou International – Five-Ram Statue." The Peoplé Government of Guangzhou Municipality, 2010. http://english.gz.gov.cn/publicfiles/business/htmlfiles/gzgoven/s9224/201104/788583.html.
5. "Informational Signs"
6. The People's Government of Guangzhou Municipality, "Guangzhou International..."
7. Le, Yangyang. 2010 Asiad mascot. Digital, April 28, 2008. http://news.dayoo.com/guangzhou/news/2008-04/28/content_3378538.htm.
8. Graff, David A., and Robin Higham, eds. *A Military History of China*. Update Edition. Lexington: The University of Kentucky, 2012.
9. "Informational Signs"
10. Graff and Higham, *A Military History of China*, 1-324
11. "Informational Signs"
12. Yi, Chu Wang. "Sun Yat-Sen." Encyclopaedia Britannica. Encycolopaedia Britannica, May 12, 2014. http://www.britannica.com/EBchecked/topic/573697/Sun-Yat-sen.
13. Graff and Higham, *A Military History of China*, 1-324
14. Yi, "Sun Yat-Sen"
15. Wilson, Tracy, and Holly Frey. Boxer Rebellion. Audio. Stuff You Missed in History Class. Accessed May 29, 2013. www.missedinhistory.com/podcast/boxer-rebellion/.
16. Graff and Higham, *A Military History of China*, 1-324
17. ibid.

18. ibid.
19. Yi, "Sun Yat-Sen"
20. Graff and Higham, *A Military History of China*, 1-324
21. Yi, "Sun Yat-Sen"
22. Graff and Higham, *A Military History of China*, 1-324
23. Yi, "Sun Yat-Sen"
24. Graff and Higham, *A Military History of China*, 1-324
25. Yi, "Sun Yat-Sen"
26. Graff and Higham, *A Military History of China*, 1-324
27. ibid.
28. Yi, "Sun Yat-Sen"
29. Graff and Higham, *A Military History of China*, 1-324
30. ibid.
31. National Geographic. *National Geographic Atlas of China: An Expansive Portrait of China Today with More than 400 Maps and Illustrations*. 1st ed. Washington D.C.: National Geographic, 2007.
32. Yi, "Sun Yat-Sen"
33. National Geographic, *National Geographic Atlas of China*, 1-128
34. "Informational Signs"
35. Guangzhou Museum. "Guangzhou Museum: Since 1929 a pamphlet." Guangzhou Museum, 2013.
36. Graff and Higham, *A Military History of China*, 1-324
37. Guangzhou Museum, "Guangzhou Museum…"
38. Graff and Higham, *A Military History of China*, 1-324
39. Guangzhou Museum, "Guangzhou Museum…"

40. Hui, Pan, and Richard Glauert. "The Kapok: Guangzhou's City Flower." Life of Guangzhou, March 25, 2013. www.lifeofgaungzhou.com/node_981/ node_989/node_996/node_1011/2013/03/ 25/1364196849139479.sh tml.
41. Guangzhou Museum, "Guangzhou Museum…"
42. Sylong Digital. "Introduction to the Museum." Guangzhou Museum Group, 2013. http://www.guangzhoumuseum.cn/en/ gbintro1.asp.
43. Guangzhou Museum, "Guangzhou Museum…"
44. Sylong Digital, "Introduction to the Museum"

Chapter 6 – Baiyun Mountain Reserve

1. TravelChinaGuide.com. "White Cloud Mountain." TravelChinaGuide.com, 1998. http://www.travelchinaguide.com/attraction/ guangdong/guangzhou/whitecloud.htm.
2. Daniell, James. "Sichuan 2008: A Disaster on an Immense Scale." May 9, 2013, sec. Science & Environment.
3. Rand McNally and Company. *Rand McNally Illustrated Atlas of China*. 1st ed. Chicago: Rand McNally, 1972.
4. Downs, Jacques M. *The Golden Ghetto*. 1st ed. London: Associated University Press, 1997.
5. Fairbank, John King, and Merle Goldman. *China: A New History; Second Enlarged Edition (2006)*. 2nd ed. Cambridge: The Belknap Press of Harvard University Press, 1992.

6. "Informational Signs: Signs at the Site Provided Facts and Details Which Were Useful in the Understanding of the Size and History of the Site," n.d.
7. ibid.
8. World Weather Online. "Guangzhou Monthly Climate Average, China." World Wearther Online, 2014. http://www.worldweatheronline.com/Guangzhou-weather-averages/Guangdong/CN.aspx.
9. "Informational Signs"
10. ibid.
11. Zhu, Beijing. "Chinese Dragon vs Western Dragon." ChinaDaily. May 31, 2013, sec. Language.
12. "Informational Signs"
13. ibid.
14. Lambert, Katie, and Sara Dowdy. How the Opium Wars Worked. Audio. Stuff You Missed in History Class. Accessed November 14, 2009. www.missedinhistory.com/podcasts/how-the-opium-wars-worked.
15. Fairbank and Merle, *China: A New History*, 1-80
16. Lambert and Dowdy, How the Opium Wars Worked, Audio
17. Wilson, Tracy, and Holly Frey. Boxer Rebellion. Audio. Stuff You Missed in History Class. Accessed May 29, 2013. www.missedinhistory.com/podcast/boxer-rebellion/.
18. Faure, David. *Emperor and Ancestory: State and Lineage in South China.* 1st ed. Stanford, California: Stanford University Press, 2007.
19. Lambert and Dowdy, How the Opium Wars Worked, Audio
20. Faure, *Emperor and Ancestory*, 1-464

21. "Informational Signs"
22. ibid.
23. ibid.
24. US National Geospatial-Intelligence Agency. "Fokien: China." ITA - Information Technology Associates, 1995. http://www.geographic.org/geographic_names/name.php?uni=-2628013&fid=1227&c=china.
25. World Health Organization. "Leprosy Elimination." WHO - World Health Organization, 2014. www.who.int/lep/transmission/en/.
26. TravelChinaGuide.com. "Qingming Festival (Tomb-sweeping Day)," 2015. Accessed June 19, 2015. http://www.travelchinaguide.com/essential/holidays/qingming.htm

Chapter 7 – Chimelong Safari Park

1. Chimelong Safari Park PR department. "Chimelong Safari Park." Chimelong Safari Park PR Department, 2014.
2. "Informational Signs: Signs at the Site Provided Facts and Details Which Were Useful in the Understanding of the Size and History of the Site," n.d.
3. Chimelong Safari Park PR department, "Chimelong Safari Park"
4. "Informational Signs"
5. Chimelong Safari Park PR department, "Chimelong Safari Park"
6. "Informational Signs"
7. Chimelong Safari Park PR department, "Chimelong Safari Park"

8. "Informational Signs"
9. Chimelong Safari Park PR department, "Chimelong Safari Park"
10. Kent, Jane. "A Mammoth Task: Carving out a Future without Illegal Ivory." That's PRD, February 2014.
11. ibid.
12. "Informational Signs"
13. Kent, "A Mammoth Task…"
14. National Zoo with the Smithsonian Institution. "Giant Pandas: Facts." Smithsonian Institution: www.si.edu, 2014. nationalzoo.si.edu/Animals/GiantPandas/PandaFacts/.
15. "Informational Signs"
16. ibid.
17. Wilson, Tracy, and Holly Frey. <u>Missed in History: Ruth Harkness and Giant Pandas</u>. Audio. Stuff You Missed in History Class. Accessed June 15, 2014. http://www.missedinhistory.com/podcasts/ruth-harkness-and-the-first-panda-in-the-u-s/.
18. Magnier, Mark. "Attack of the Pandas." Los Angeles Times. March 21, 2006, sec. Foreign Relations. articles.latimes.com/2006/mar/21/world/fg-pandas21.
19. "Informational Signs"
20. ibid.
21. ibid.
22. ibid.
23. ibid.
24. Fasman, Jon. "Food for Thought: Taste for Rare, Wild Pangolin Is Driving the Mammal to Extinction." NPR.org. August 3, 2014.

25. "Informational Signs"
26. ibid.